AN AUTHOR'S GUIDE
TO PUBLISHING
BETTER ARTICLES
IN BETTER JOURNALS
IN THE BEHAVIORAL
SCIENCES

AN AUTHOR'S GUIDE TO PUBLISHING BETTER ARTICLES IN BETTER JOURNALS IN THE BEHAVIORAL SCIENCES

Joel Kupfersmid
and
Donald M. Wonderly

Clinical Psychology Publishing Co., Inc.
4 Conant Square
Brandon, Vermont 05733

Copyright © 1994 by Clinical Psychology Publishing Company, Inc., Brandon, Vermont.

Library of Congress Catalog Card Number: 93–71124

ISBN: 0–88422–123–7

CPPC   4 Conant Square
         Brandon, Vermont 05733

Cover design: Sue Thomas

Printed in the United States of America.

CONTENTS

1 DISSATISFACTION WITH RESEARCH REPORTING

This book addresses the problem of dissatisfaction experienced by many who publish in psychology and education journals. It is assumed that most behavioral scientists desire to write quality papers, documents that will be noticed and respected by others in the field. Our purpose is to attempt to reduce the proportion of articles that are considered to be inept. The audience should be—primarily—behavioral scientists who have published and want to improve the content of their articles, or who have not yet published but want to author papers with substance.

This book is not intended for beginning researchers or others who are unfamiliar with experimental techniques, conducting literature reviews, and writing manuscripts in APA style. There are a variety of good books and articles in each of these areas. Neither is it intended for those professionals who must publish, regardless of quality, in order to be hired, keep their jobs, and/or attain tenure or promotion.

The Problem

Data from a variety of sources suggest that both practitioners and experimental psychologists are displeased with the content of articles in their professional journals. Lindsey (1977) asked: "How is it that so much triviality, illiteracy, and dullness is yearly entered into the scientific publication stream?" Mahoney (1976) claimed that "many scientific journals have seriously retarded our progress by absurd, inefficient, and often prejudicial policies." Nelson (1982) added that "most published manuscripts will be soon forgotten by editors, reviewers, and the general reader because they are eminently forgettable" (p. 229). Evidence supporting Nelson's position comes from studies on an article's "impact factor" (i.e., the extent to which a paper is referenced in other articles).

Garvey and Griffith (1971) reported that 50% of all research articles are read by approximately 1% of psychologists. These same researchers (1979) noted that in their investigation of over 200 research studies conducted by psychologists, only one study in seven originated from the investigator's reading a journal article or listening to a research presentation. Similarly, Matson, Gouvier, and Manikam (1989) found that the mean citation rate is less than one (0.92) per published article across psychology journals. One journal reviewer lamented that "one would like to think that if scientists were content with what is currently being published, they would pay more attention to it (cite it) when they write their own papers" (anonymous personal communication, September 11, 1987). Mahoney (1985) concluded that "the motivation to read seems to fall far short of the motivation to publish" (p. 31).

Surveys of mental health practitioners' attitudes toward the quality of what is published display considerable inconsistency. On the positive side, when asked what the best source of research information useful to their work is, mental health administrators and research members of grant review committees ($N = 147$) rated professional journal articles at the top of the list (Weiss & Bucuvalas, 1980). Similarly, when psychologists employed at V.A. hospitals, medical schools, state hospitals, mental health centers, and in private practice ($N = 224$) rank ordered the usefulness of eight sources of information, research articles were rated third on the list (Cohen, 1979).

However, more recent studies indicate that many mental health practitioners are dissatisfied with the content of their professional journals. In Thelen and Rodriquez's (1987) sample of clinical psychologists ($N = 379$), only 42% reported that research is useful in clinical practice. Similarly, 37% of Morrow-Bradley and Elliot's (1986) sample of psychotherapists ($N = 279$) claimed that journal articles were useful. When these same authors asked their sample to rank order nine sources of information in terms of usefulness, reading psychotherapy research and doing psychotherapy research were rated eighth and ninth, respectively. Rank ordering of the usefulness of eight information resources by child therapists ($N = 30$) parallels the above findings. For child psychotherapists, empirical articles and empirical books were rated seventh and eighth, respectively (Cohen, Sargent, & Sechrest, 1986). Morrow-

Bradley and Elliot (1986) concluded that "with virtual unanimity, psychotherapy researchers have argued that (a) psychotherapy research should yield information useful to practicing therapists, (b) such research to date has not done so, and (c) this problem should be remedied" (p. 188). Barlow (1981) contended that "at present, clinical research has little or no influence on clinical practice" (p. 147). A stronger indictment was offered by Meehl (1978):

> Most so-called "theories" in the soft areas of psychology (clinical, counseling, social, personality, community, and school psychology) are scientifically unimpressive and technologically worthless. In soft psychology theories rise and decline, come and go, more as a function of baffled boredom than anything else; and the enterprise shows a disturbing absence of that *cumulative* character. (pp. 806–807)

Surveys and comments of experimental psychologists also indicate considerable vexation with what is published. Only 15% of the surveyed members of the Society of Experimental Social Psychology ($N = 229$), an elite subgroup of social psychologists, believe that existing criteria for evaluating research are appropriate (Lewicki, 1982). Perhaps more distressing are the findings reported by Ward, Hall, and Schramm (1975). These researchers had judges rate the quality of 114 *published* articles with the author's name and affiliation removed. All judges were members of the Division of Measurement and Research Methodology of the American Educational Research Association. In only 40% of the articles reviewed from education journals would the judges have accepted for publication the article as submitted or with minor revisions needed. The remaining 60% of articles were judged to require major revisions (33%) or outright rejection for publication (26%). Results were not much better for psychology journals. The judges rated 43% of these articles as publishable in the form in which they were submitted, or requiring only minor revisions, whereas the remaining 57% required major revisions (29%) or deserved outright rejection (28%).

Former editor of the *Journal of Comparative and Physiological Psychology* Harry Harlow (1962) has been vocal in his frustration over the contents of articles published in research journals. He wrote that:

> most experiments are not worth doing and the data obtained are not worth publishing. . . . Faced with a mounting flood of

uninspired researches and watching publication lag continuously mount. . . . I have the rubber stamp which I planned to use on a large number of manuscripts: "Not read but rejected." (p. 896)

Discontent with journal articles is evident in other disciplines as well. A sociologist and former editor of *Social Problems* wrote to his replacement that "if you can keep your head above the inundation of trivial manuscripts, you will glory in the occasional manuscript of brilliance" (Rodman, 1970, p. 269). Another sociologist (McCartney, 1976) believes "the most critical question we ought to ask is how the present system [of journal publication]. . . . serves the knowledge needs of the discipline. On this score, sociology journals deserve their lowest marks" (p. 147). Even among physicists there are rumblings about journal article quality. Cole (1991) reports the overwhelming majority of articles published in physics journals are rarely cited. A survey of physicists in England concluded that "*all* our respondents thought that the vast majority of papers in the journals which they read were of poor quality or of little significance" (p. 140).

Some of the most blunt criticism about journal content has come from the medical community. With specific reference to biomedical journals, Broad and Wade (1982a) claimed that "too many simply worthless scientific articles are published. Such publications not only prevent good research from receiving the attention it deserves, they also indirectly protect bad research from scrutiny by cluttering up the communications system of science" (p. 50). The current editor of the *Journal of the American Medical Association*, Drummond Rennie (1986), leaves little room for ambiguity about his position:

> There seems to be no study too fragmented, no hypothesis too trivial, no literature citation too biased or too egotistical, no design too warped, no methodology too bungled, no presentation of results too inaccurate, too obscure, and too contradictory, no analysis too self-serving, no argument too circular, no conclusion too trifling or too unjustified, and no grammar and syntax too offensive for a paper to end up in print. (p. 2391)

Writing in the *Journal of Behavioral and Brain Sciences*, Tyrer (1991) offers the most pithy analysis thus far stated: "A determined author can get any rubbish published" (p. 164).

These findings suggest that many psychologists, regardless of specialization (as well as many other scientists from a broad range of disciplines), believe that a high percentage of articles published in their professional journals are uninteresting, uninformative, irrelevant, and not likely to contribute to the accumulation of scientific knowledge. The reasons for this widespread discontent with much of what is published in professional journals should be considered relative to the dynamics motivating many professionals to publish.

The Motivation for Publishing

There is a tacit presumption that behavioral scientists across the country are studying psychological and educational phenomena in laboratories and clinics in order to advance the progress of science. It is assumed that these investigators must be addressing important concerns related to psychological processes and are collecting data that will aid in answering critical questions. When authors of articles in the *Journal of Consulting and Clinical Psychology* ($N = 333$) were asked why they publish, 88% reported that it was for the purpose of following up on some previously published research (Kendall & Ford, 1979). Although this may be an accurate assessment, some believe that the basic reason for publishing often rests on less laudable motives. Mahoney (1985) contended:

> While the ends sought through publication can be rationalized in terms of advancing thought and knowledge of a discipline, it is likely that publication is primarily motivated by personal ends of the producer. By and large, scholars are seeking enhancement of their personal reputations for the purposes of achieving tenure, increased salaries, job offers from other employers, and support for their research endeavors. (p. 20)

Bracey (1987) echoed these sentiments: "We seem to be headed toward a situation where 'knowledge production' (as they like to call it in universities) is an exercise in solipsism. The chief beneficiary is the author, who gets promotions, tenure, prestige, and more grants to write more stuff that won't be read" (p. 44).

Psychologists are human beings. As such, they often do first what profits themselves. Those trained in experimental and other primarily research-oriented areas of psychology have limited opportunities for jobs beyond that of university employment. Thus, an experimental psychologist is captive to the standards set by universities in general, and psychology departments in particular. For practitioner psychologists desiring employment in a university setting, the same vocational dynamics apply.

The main criterion for being hired in many departments of psychology is the number of publications a candidate has produced, and it is not unusual for a young professor to want to remain at his or her place of employment after being hired. Being allowed to retain one's university position usually involves securing tenure. Again, the main criterion is the extent to which an individual has published since being hired. The next assignment a professor seeks is the supervision of graduate—preferably doctoral—students. Often the major criterion used to assess a professor's skills in this area is the extent to which he or she has published (Mahoney, 1976).

> It is in the realms of publication and academic employment that we confront some of the most powerful selection processes in contemporary science. Publication, for example, lies at the very heart of modern academic science—at levels ranging from the epistemic certification of scientific thought to the more personal labyrinths of job security, quality of life, and self-esteem.... Teaching excellence, creative thinking, and all manner of other valuable attributes will do little to earn security in academic science if they are not accompanied by published payment to the piper of tenure. (Mahoney, 1985, p. 30)

Thus, although it is often assumed that university faculty are hired to teach and are heavily evaluated in this skill, the major factor determining professorial longevity at many universities is the extent to which one has articles in print (Boyer, 1990). In a national survey of university professors, 40% reported that at their university the number of publications supersedes the quality of the articles in determining tenure (Boyer, 1990).

In addition to job security and advancement, it is normal to want to be recognized in one's professional field. Mahoney (1976) listed the six most common forms of recognition a scientist can achieve:

1. Being invited to speak at professional presentations or to write articles for professional publications.

2. Having one's work cited in another's published paper.
3. Having grant proposals approved for funding.
4. Being offered employment at a more prestigious institution.
5. Receiving a special award for scientific achievement.
6. Having one's name associated with a phenomenon (e.g., Spearman rank order correlation, Thurstone scale).

Essential to achievement of any of these six forms of recognition is that the individual has published. It would be very unlikely for a scientist to be asked to speak or write an article, be cited in another's work, or receive special awards without having his or her work appear in print. For the same reason, one of the criteria for receiving a grant is that the submitter can document a fertile history of research experience. Likewise, to have one's name associated with a phenomenon (eponymity) almost universally requires one to have published its discovery. Being offered employment at a higher status university is frequently a function of one's publication history. Ghiselin (1989) maintained that "of course good teaching ought to be rewarded, but in academia its official recognition is little more than a public-relations gesture" (p. 71).

"Faculty research brings state, regional, and national visibility to academic institutions. It becomes a means whereby an institution can establish a reputation for outstanding faculty and demonstrate achievement and progress to the public" (Creswell, 1985, p. 1). When a scientist publishes in a professional journal, the article almost always includes the author's name and *institutional affiliation*. As a means of reducing the emphasis that is placed on publications in university settings, Tighe (1979) proposed that professors be allowed time to conduct research, with the proviso that the product not be submitted for publication until after the author's death. He termed this policy "perish and publish."

The "publish or perish" criterion is probably most pronounced in universities housing doctoral programs. In Kendall and Ford's (1979) study asking authors of articles their primary reason for engaging in research, 35% of the sample reported that conducting experiments was part of their job requirement. Creswell (1985) concluded his review of the dynamics surrounding the motivation to publish with the observation that little can be done to encourage those not interested in publishing and little can be engendered to stop those interested in publishing. Boice and Jones (1984) provided some support for this conclusion. They reported that about 10% of the scientists in a given discipline account for approximately 50% of the published literature. It may well be that the majority of professors attempt to meet the minimum requirements of publications necessary for job security, tenure, and advancement.

In essence, for a great number of those publishing, *quantity* may well supersede *quality*. Mahoney (1979) contended that "as long as personal advancement depends on publication, we can expect scientists to display behaviours which are more expediently aimed towards their advancement, rather than that of knowledge" (p. 365). President of the Association of American Universities Robert Rosenzweig noted that scientists may have an image problem: "Mr. Chips has been replaced by Dr. Faustus, an ambitious, hard-driving entrepreneur, whose research, teaching and personal economic interests are very hard to disentangle" (Adler, 1989, p. 5).

In an effort to curb the proliferation of articles written for the purpose of meeting some university and/or academic departmental criterion for self-promotion, Stanford University president Donald Kennedy has instituted a new way of assessing the publication product of his faculty. Stanford University now gives cash bonuses for good teaching. Additionally, those applying for promotion are limited in the number of publications they are allowed to submit for evaluation. The authoring of textbooks will be on an equal footing with articles in professional journals (Gordon, 1991).

For many scientists the "university game" is publish, publish, publish. It behooves the researcher to know how to conduct experiments (a skill presumably learned in graduate school), and to learn the criteria by which journal editors and reviewers make a differential determination of the publishability of each manuscript submitted (a craft usually learned during the pre-tenurial years). Because large numbers of individuals *must* publish to obtain a desired position, *must* publish to retain their position, and often *have to* publish to advance in the position, the quantity of publications rather than their quality becomes the greater concern.

"The Big Picture"

Mahoney (1987) stated: "There are over 40,000 current scientific journals, publishing 2 new articles per minute (2,800 per day and over one million per year), and this rate has been doubling about every six years" (p. 165). There are approximately 300 journals of a psychological and/or educational nature (American Psychological Association, 1988), and about 8,000 medical journals (Broad & Wade, 1982b). Given the sheer number of professional journals, getting a manuscript published is not difficult. However, the task of writing a quality paper that advances one's discipline and having that paper published in a "better" journal can be formidable. Many empirical and quasi-empirical investigations related to the journal publication process will be reviewed in this book. There is within the domain of metascience a process termed "scientific evaluation" which involves assessing the quality of science and suggesting alterations that might improve its operation (Shadish, 1989b). This text may, thus, be appropriately considered a form of scientific evaluation.

2 CAUSES OF DISSATISFACTION: HYPOTHESIS TEST AND NEGATIVE RESULTS BIAS

The need to publish in the interest of professional survival dilutes the possible contribution of the scientific community. However, the approach to data analysis employed by most researchers, as well as the nature of editorial/peer reviewer bias in the manuscript acceptance/ rejection process, adds a dimension that has resulted in an unnecessary distortion of the scientific knowledge bank.

Statistical Significance Bias

It is virtually axiomatic that if one hopes to publish a study based on some form of statistical analysis (e.g., t test, ANOVA, correlation coefficient), an associated p value must accompany the data. That p value is used to determine whether to retain or reject a null hypothesis. For over 30 years editors have been publishing criticisms about the use of significance testing. Yet such testing persists as the preeminent form of data analysis. However, when we attempted to locate, in professional journals, articles supporting its use, only a few papers were found.

Those who argue for the use of statistical significance testing as the primary means of hypothesis testing do so for a variety of reasons. Thus, the debate on this topic involves a number of issues, such as the use of a p value as a decision-making tool, problems associated with the interpretation of p values, etc. Our position is that the use of any predetermined p value for the purpose of making a decision regarding whether to retain or reject a (null or experimental) hypothesis is inappropriate.

We believe that the reporting of p values is essential. However, we reject the establishment of a preset alpha level as the major factor in determining whether an experimental outcome is to be considered a chance or nonchance event.

The documents reviewed provide three major reasons for recommending reliance on significance tests. The first argument was offered by Mohr (1990), who contended:

> We are in most cases not far enough along theoretically to be concerned with the range in which an estimated value probably lies; we just want to know whether or not a certain relationship or other quantity is worth further thought. (p. 8)

This position rests on several questionable suppositions. First, it is assumed that a more advanced theory needs to be developed before the behavioral sciences should be permitted to measure variables more precisely. The opposite argument to that of Mohr's can be offered. More adequate theories in the behavioral sciences will come to fruition when more suitable means of measuring variables are utilized.

Hedges (1987) noted that the behavioral sciences are usually considered "soft" (i.e., there is less of a cumulative aspect to the data generated) when compared to the natural sciences. He distinguished two types of cumulativeness. Theoretical cumulativeness is a function of "empirical laws and theoretical structures built on one another so that later developments extend and unify earlier work. The assessment of theoretical cumulativeness must be rather subjective" (p. 443). According to Hedges, a more objective approach is *empirical* cumulativeness, which is the degree to which there is agreement across experiments that makes conceptual sense in a given area of study. He then compared the consistency of experimental results across several subdisciplines of psychology with that of particle physics.

The measurement of data consistency commonly employed in the physical sciences is Birge's ratio, which is similar to a chi square test of goodness of fit. Both tests express in quantitative terms how well data from a set of studies agree, and for both tests, the larger the number the greater the inconsistency of results across studies.

The Particle Data Group (an elite group of physicists) publishes a comprehensive review of stable particles, including their masses and lifetimes. Outcomes are available for 13 quantitative reviews that include at least 10 studies per review. When all studies are subjected to analysis

(N = 181), Birge's ratio = 2.11. To compare the consistency of psychological research with that in physics, Hedges selected 11 areas of psychology (e.g., sex differences in spatial ability, sex differences in verbal ability, effects of open education on achievement and self-concept) which included 13 reviews. When all reviews were analyzed, the average Birge's ratio for the data was 2.09. Returning to Mohr's contentions, it is difficult to determine whether he believed that particle physics is not sufficiently advanced to employ parameter estimations or whether the behavioral sciences have the sophistication to go beyond use of significance tests.

Although a debate could go on about the relative scientific status of the behavioral sciences, Mohr's further statements regarding the appropriateness of the procedure seemed to settle the issue. Fifty-two pages after stating that psychology is not sufficiently advanced to go beyond the use of significance tests, he stated "obviously, interval estimation is a better way, and everybody knows and says that it should be used more, but it is more trouble" (p. 60).

In one aside, Mohr negated any possible argument he had previously made regarding the usefulness of significance tests, with the excuse that they are less trouble to use. For whom this procedure is less trouble was not stated. But, more important, what kind of reasoning was being employed? He was apparently suggesting that data analysis should be accomplished with the easiest method regardless of suitability. His position is probably one of the strongest arguments for *not* utilizing significance tests that we have been able to locate.

The second argument supporting the use of significance tests over other forms of data analysis was presented by Chow (1988). He contended that the use of statistics measuring parameter estimates and strength of relationships is suitable for descriptive research, but significance tests are appropriate for experiments that attempt to corroborate explanatory theories. Chow proposed that in corroborative studies the goal is to choose among two or more rival hypotheses and that significance tests are an objective form of binary decision making well-suited for this process.

Henkel (1976), in an earlier paper, had taken strong issue with Chow's position: "The tests [of statistical significance] are of little value or no value in basic social science research, where basic research is identified as that which is directed toward the development and validation of theory" (p. 7). He took the position that statistical significance testing in any given study is a single isolated event that only answers "yes" or "no" to whether one can believe that the outcome was a chance occurrence. (But who should believe it? The researcher? Other scientists? Consumers?)

> Thus, the believers in the utility of tests of significance are in the peculiar position of either having to repeat the test of significance for a particular hypothesis whenever someone wishes to know whether the hypothesis is true or false, or having to concede that a single test of the hypothesis determines once and for all time the truth or falsity of a hypothesis. Surely most researchers would find either solution unacceptable, but to do so implies that the test of significance is essentially irrelevant to the purpose of basic scientific research. (p. 85)

Meehl (1978) argued that continual reliance on significance testing is antithetical to any attempt at providing an accumulative data base. "Since the null hypothesis is quasi-always false . . . 'significant differences' are little more than complex, causally uninterpretable outcomes of statistical power functions" (p. 806).

Dooling and Danks (1975) claimed that significance testing can answer the question of whether a variable has an effect, although they agree that it says nothing about the strength of that variable. But having an "effect" seems to assume some *meaningful* strength. For example, two variables that are correlated to the extent that $r = .01$ with $p < .0001$, would be considered to be highly statistically significantly related. But, how many researchers would consider that an "effect" had been discovered?

Morrison and Henkel (1969) stated that the only way one can rationally decide on a reasonable p value is in situations where the cost of a wrong decision can be determined. Since this is virtually never met in comparing rival hypotheses, to predetermine a p value of .05 is "to talk about the science of business, not the business of science" (p. 137).

Some authors, like Chow (1988), claim that the significance test is not a decision factor, being no more than a judgmental element. Rozeboom (1960) agreed that decision making is not the primary focus of individual empirical investigation. He contended that *the primary aim of a scientific experiment is not to precipitate decisions, but to make an appropriate adjustment in the degree to which one accepts, or believes, the hypothesis*" (p. 420). He added that the scientist's task "is not to prescribe actions, but to establish rational beliefs upon which to base them" (p. 422). Bakan (1966) offered the disclaimer that research psychologists do not usually deal with practical contexts. They are "rather interested in making assertions concerning psychological functions which have a reasonable amount of credibility associated with them. [They are] more concerned with 'what is the case' than with 'what is it wise to do' " (pp. 159–160).

Morrison and Henkel (1969/1970) took a similar position, saying that "in the vast majority of instances in which significance tests are reported in behavioral research no firm decision is required because no specific actions are to be guided by the decisions" (p. 310). However, many writers have taken pains to demonstrate that statistical analysis is intimately related to decision making. Freund (1960), for example, said, *"A major task of modern statistics is . . . to provide criteria which minimize the chances of making wrong decisions"* (p. 239). Richmond (1964) stated that "a test of a hypothesis is a procedure for choosing between two alternative courses of action" (p. 166). Why make the determination that a tomato is ripe *enough* unless one is deciding whether it should be picked, sold, or eaten? If no decisions are ultimately involved, why do research? "The process of ratiocination and the conviction of the veracity of . . . judgments refers to an ability . . . to draw a particular type of conclusion" (Wonderly, 1991, p. 234). Such conclusions are critical to decision making—and to the behavioral process.

Although many behavioral scientists challenge the appropriateness of statistical significance testing (or the idea of hypothesis testing in general), they consistently find a reason for allowing that under some circumstances it performs a useful function. Morrison and Henkel (1969/1970) provided an example, saying "the tests are . . . clearly applicable and useful for research contexts" (p. 310). Yet they also stated that in itself "knowledge of the level of significance does [not] provide any clue as to its theoretical or other interpretation" (p. 132). They agreed that there are many errors associated with significance testing but provided information "for the improved *use* of significance tests" [italics added] (p. 139). Lykken (1968/1970) confessed that "the finding of statistical significance is *perhaps the least important* attribute of a good experiment" [italics added] (p. 278). He apparently believed that it is of some importance, however.

Cowles and Davis (1982) agreed that "the point at which . . . rejection occurs depends largely on . . . how it is interpreted by each individual" (p. 557). However, they drew the conclusion that to the extent people believe "an event which occurs 5% of the time or less is a rare event [and are] prepared to ascribe a cause other than mere chance to such infrequent events . . . the adoption of the level as a criterion for judging outcomes is justifiable" (p. 557). Greenwald (1975) agreed, even attempting to "make a positive case for the formulation of more potent and acceptable null hypotheses as a part of an overall research strategy" (p. 1).

Salsburg (1985) said that most people "recognize the *limited* value of hypothesis testing" (p. 223), but the degree to which it is employed suggests otherwise. Carver (1978), who supports our view and "recommend[s] abandoning all statistical significance testing" (p. 378), spoke at one point, however, of "the small *benefits* there might be to using statistical significance testing" [italics added] (p. 397). He finally suggested that the abandonment of such testing for graduate school students "should be seriously considered" (p. 396).

Even Rozeboom (1960), who made a strong case against significance testing (over 30 years ago!) said only that it (the significance test) "is *seldom* if ever appropriate to the aims of scientific research" [italics added] (p. 417). He made the astonishing statement that "[people] have never taken the method seriously anyway" (p. 424).

One of the most disconcerting aspects of statistical significance testing is that, in the case of nondirectional hypotheses, there are *always* some differences between groups and *some* relationships between variables. No two groups of subjects or variables are effectively equal; rather, statistically significant difference will always be discovered if the researcher has a large enough sample N. "The question is *never* whether the result is statistically significant, but rather, at what N the data would reach statistical significance" (Kupfersmid, 1988, p. 636). Bakan (1966) made the same point, stating that "there *is really no good reason to expect the null hypothesis to be true in any population* [and] a sufficiently large number of observations will lead to [its] rejection" (p. 150).

Suppose one compared the scores of large numbers of students, all of whom were identified as "visual learners" and who had been randomly assigned to two types of reading program. Group A used a visual instruction approach to reading, while Group B employed an auditory approach. The explanatory rival theories being tested would be whether a visual or auditory approach resulted in better reading among visual learners. If there was only a 2% difference on a standardized reading test between Group A's performance versus Group B's performance (e.g., using national norms, the median score for Group A is at the 52nd percentile, the median score for Group B is at the 50th percentile) and this was statistically significant ($p < .01$), the data would corroborate/support one of the rival theories (the visual approach). Would a school be advised to implement the program received by Group A for visual learners regardless of the differences in cost between the two programs, teacher training time required, etc.?

Like Mohr, Chow (1988) agreed with the problem posed by such data, thus negating his own position: "It is true that a statistical test will be significant if a large enough sample is used. On the other hand, any test may be made insignificant if too few subjects are tested" (p. 109). Another example of the propensity of proponents of statistical significance testing for challenging their own positions!

Dooling and Danks (1975) provided a third rationale for the continued use of significance tests. They believed that the procedure is appropriate for the analysis of correlations and similar statistics. However, they eschewed statistical analyses that determine the proportion of accounted-for variance and, presumably, analysis of effect size. "Our quarrel," they said, "is . . . with the possible (and we think, probable) misinterpretation of the proportion of variance accounted-for measure" (p. 15).

> The crux of our argument is that in the experimental designs typically employed by psychologists, the selection of the levels of the independent variable is not sufficiently well defined to permit legitimate inferences about the strength of that independent variable's effect. [T]he *E* typically employs the fixed-effects model in his analysis [and] cannot then legitimately generalize the results of his analysis to all conceivable levels of the independent variable. Consequently, [proportion of accounted-for variance] appropriately describes only the strength of the *particular* levels of the independent variable on the dependent variable, not the influence of the independent variable *in general*. . . . By far, the greatest number of research designs used in psychology limit the scope of the experiment to the question: "Does this variable have an effect?" A test of significance is entirely adequate for answering such a question. Most analysis of variance experiments in psychology are not designed to provide information on the further question: "How strongly are these two variables related?" (pp. 16–17)

Dooling and Dank's concern that a statistic might be misinterpreted or overgeneralized is sound. It would not be advantageous to use statistical techniques where implications are not understood. It is not clear whether proportion of variance accounted for is difficult for behavioral scientists to understand. However, there is considerable evidence that the interpretation of p values, and rejection levels, is often misconceived.

Bakan's (1966) and Carver's (1978) analysis of the interpretation of p values in statistical textbooks and in the literature indicates that p values are often misunderstood to mean (a) the degree of probability that the results were due to chance, (b) the probability of obtaining the same results upon experimental replication, or (c) the probability that the research hypothesis is true. "The p value may be used to make a decision about accepting or rejecting the idea that chance caused the results. This is what statistical significance testing is—nothing more, nothing less" (Carver, 1978, p. 387). The argument that if a statistic can be misinterpreted it should be prohibited should, as we are suggesting, lead to the disqualification of all significance testing.

Dooling and Danks (1975) were, understandably, concerned with the generalizability that researchers might make about outcomes from most experiments. They worried that behavioral scientists may overextend the range of effects that an independent variable may cover. Thus, they advised, it is better to "play it safe" and make a more conservative statement regarding whether a likely nonchance event has occurred. (Of course it, and every other approach, will show a nonchance effect if the N is sufficiently large and the variance sufficiently small.)

A rebuttal to Dooling and Dank's position on this issue relates to the implicit assumption that some behavioral scientists may jump to sweeping conclusions on the basis of one—or very few—studies. If this were true, the problem would be one of education rather than an inherent limitation of statistical significance tests. It is widely accepted that no one study can be definitive because no single study can possibly assess the full range of effects any independent variable may have. It is the accumulation of effects that a range of independent variables has on a dependent variable across many subject samples and conditions that leads to credible generalizations. Almost all individual studies are limited in the range of values that the independent variable is able to assume, but that limitation may be mitigated if literature reviews of a particular area are conducted.

It should be understood that even when a statistically significant effect/relationship is found, the logic of science precludes any claim by the researcher that the experimental hypothesis has been confirmed. Many philosophers of science have demonstrated that experimental hypotheses can never be considered confirmed, even when predicted results are obtained (i.e., when a statistically significant difference is reported). The logical statement that if P (hypothesis is correct) therefore Q (predicted outcome occurs) does not logically mean that if Q has occurred therefore P is correct. The logic of "if P then Q, Q therefore P" is faulty. One can only (logically) conclude that if Q (experimental outcome) is *not* in the predicted direction, P (experimental hypothesis) is false.

This is a logical proposition known as *modus tollens*. Although such thinking has weaknesses (e.g., scientific theories do not always predict accurately, some experimental data cannot be predicted by any current theory, there are usually no one or two clear experimental tests in which disconfirmatory data will automatically discredit an established theory, etc.), it is currently the best way to go about evaluating beliefs that are subject to the scientific methods that have been developed (Mahoney, 1976).

Some authors (like Popper) believe that although the rejection of a null hypothesis is only a tentative finding, the failure to reject gives us relatively sure data. They contend that although the scientific method is not logically capable of confirming a hypothesis, it is logically capable of disconfirming, or making less credible, a hypothesis or theory *if* the experimental outcome is not statistically significant. "Given that the logic of science should be more properly *falsificational* rather than *confirmational*, negative (or contratheoretical) results yield much more information than positive results. It is only *unsuccessful* predictions which carry conclusive logical implications" (Mahoney, 1977, p. 163).

But retention of the null hypothesis, in that it involves possible Type II errors, is no more "conclusive" than a flawed rejection. Furthermore it suggests that there is *no* difference. What of a situation in which a research study showed that the difference in mortality rates between comparable treatments for a particular disorder was only a (highly insignificant) 2%. If all costs were equal would an individual ignore the "difference"? And, if the treatment with the 2% advantage was twice as expensive would they pay the difference? Would it matter if the difference was $20 or $2,000? Would the size of the sample, the wealth of the patient, or any of an array of additional data make no difference at all? Wouldn't the patient be far better off dealing with all of the information available *with the significance test eliminated?*

We have spoken here a number of times about large and small samples. According to a number of researchers, the problem with awkward test results may be ameliorated by adjusting sample size. But what size should be chosen, considering that in some instances it is apparently "too small" and in others "too large"? Efforts have been made to make a case for a "reasonable" sample size—perhaps $N = 30$ or 40. Statisticians ordinarily refer to samples of over 30 as "large." This is where z and t distribution values coincide. More important, it is the point beyond which it is assumed that considerable confidence can be placed on the congruence of a statistic with the parameter that it is intended to represent. This attention to sample size would, however, do nothing to legitimize the use of significance tests, although increased sample sizes would reduce the incidence of Type II errors.

Among other problems with drawing inferences from research findings is that in the real world of serious research, random samples are nonexistent. Studies are done with individuals drawn from an existing pool. Even when samples are drawn with every attention to randomness, they fail to meet a basic principle of sample selection. Because the data collected are in almost every instance designed to treat a population including not yet existing individuals (e.g., individuals who may have cancer in the future), randomness cannot be achieved. Although this, in itself, may not be a critical weakness (because in such studies it is not possible to assure that every member of the relevant population has an equal opportunity to be represented), the extreme care taken to assure that researchers sample with replacement adds to the myth that what is produced (which includes significance testing) is appropriate.

It may seem that when directional hypotheses are employed, the major problem—that all (null) hypotheses will be rejected if the N is sufficiently large—has been overcome. Obviously, failure to reject such hypotheses makes no claim regarding the precise value of the estimated parameter. However, once again the issue is not resolved. Although statisticians have provided an array of arguments against the use of significance tests, the one that we are concerned with is elemental. *It is always inappropriate to establish a rejection level because there is no conceivable circumstance in which the results of a study could have the same judgmental value for all who may make use of the data.*

We are not recommending that the collection and analysis of data should be discontinued, but that if hypothesis testing cannot be eradicated, reports should display all of the relevant information and avoid the establishment of significance levels, which are always subjective, provide no useful information, and at worst lead to misleading conclusions. What we propose is no more than the elimination of a step. No more work, no more difficulty, no additional analysis is required. Information regarding sample size, collection techniques, derived statistics, the dispersion of scores around those statistics, and the probability (*p* value) associated with the occurrence of such statistics is essential. However, judgments regarding the interpretation of the data, and decisions based on such judgments, *are totally idiosyncratic*.

We conclude this section with an example of what could be a major concern for researchers. The vast majority of research studies (certainly all dissertations) are preceded by several steps. First a rationale for the study must be provided. Reasons must be given for the purpose of doing the study. What *decisions* will be affected by the outcome? What behaviors may follow? Second, a *justification* must be provided. On the basis of previous research (the "reasonableness" of expecting the treatment to have an effect), the researcher must be convinced that acceptance of the research or alternative hypothesis is to be expected.

In many cases, of course, the results of a study provide data insufficiently large to call for rejection. The *p* value associated with the data may, for example, be .10, where a .05 significance level was established at the outset. In such cases a strange conclusion must be drawn. Consider these factors:

1. Sufficient data were provided at the outset to convince the researcher—and in most cases a committee—that a difference was to be expected; that the alternative hypothesis should probably be accepted.

2. It is well known that statistics provide the best estimate of associated parameters.

3. The study in question produced a discrepancy that was still unlikely to occur by chance. The result, thus, provides evidence in favor of the argument that there is some discrepancy, though that difference may not be very large.

However, what is considered the appropriate (and, in many instances, required by university committees) interpretation of the data? The researcher is now to believe, (report) to a committee of his or her peers, *and publish if possible* the conclusion that the underlying parameter is to be found either at the null point, or, in the case of a one-tailed test, somewhere below the level necessary for rejection. It is incumbent on the researcher to ignore what reason would suggest, and to accept an interpretation that involves denying the conclusion that the data seem to indicate.

Negative Results Bias

In spite of the many weaknesses of significance testing, we must deal with current reality—with the way in which journal editors and reviewers treat research findings that fail to reject a stated hypothesis. Journal editors and reviewers are reluctant to publish negative experimental results. In fact, the *Publication Manual of the American Psychological Association* (1983) listed "reporting of negative results" as a *major* defect editors find in papers submitted for publication.

Unfortunately, scientific journals that select for publication only those manuscripts that report statistically significant outcomes doom their field of study to the pervasive problem of Type I error (rejection of a true null hypothesis) contamination. Type I errors are assumed to be more serious than Type II errors (the rejection of a true research hypothesis) because when a Type I error appears in print it may stop researchers from studying the area and/or submitting nonsignificant outcomes for publication (Bakan, 1966). Rosenthal (1979) coined this the "file drawer problem" wherein "journals are filled with the 5% of the studies that show Type I errors, while the file drawers back at the lab are filled with 95% of the studies that show nonsignificant (e.g., $p >$ .05) results" (p. 638).

Because of the strong bias against publishing negative outcomes, two extremely critical aspects of the scientific enterprise are compromised. Without the publication of negative results, a hypothesis is not subject to disproof. Second, if only studies that report statistically significant findings are published, it is difficult to determine whether a phenomenon exists or simply is a chance occurrence (Type I error) caused by journal editor selection bias. This is bound to wreak havoc when an attempt is made to conduct a literature review.

The degree of editor/reviewer bias against publishing negative results, and the effect this has on authors' behaviors regarding what papers to submit for publication, has been investigated in two ways. Peer reviewers for three Canadian journals of psychology ($N = 193$) were asked to list manuscript characteristics that had the greatest effect on whether the paper would be accepted or rejected for publication. Twenty percent of the respondents noted that if no statistically significant outcomes were reported the recommendation would be to reject the manuscript (Rowney & Zenisek, 1980).

Editors and reviewers of 19 management journals ($N = 283$) were less kind toward publishing negative findings. Of this group, 71% reported that they would reject any paper that tested a new theory and failed to find some statistically significant effect. This may be understandable in that there may be a lot of outlandish theories being tested. However, 48% of this sample had the same opinion about publishing a paper testing a theory of current interest to the field where the outcome was to retain the null hypothesis (Kerr, Tolliver, & Petree, 1977). The editors of *Science* (1992) magazine say quite frankly that to be accepted for publication "research articles . . . are expected to contain new data representing a major breakthrough in [their] field" (p. 36). Obviously no replication study, nor any in which the null is retained, would be accepted under such editorial policies, making it almost impossible to evaluate the strength of support or nonsupport for any theory.

Researchers are acutely aware of journal editor/reviewer bias against publishing negative results. Greenwald (1975) reported that his sample of behavioral scientists ($N = 81$) claimed there is a 50% chance they would submit a paper for publication if the results of an experiment were statistically significant. If the outcome was nonsignificant, only 6% would submit. Coursol and Wagner (1986) asked members of APA Division 12 (Clinical Psychology) and Division 17 (Counseling Psychology) if they had ever conducted a psychotherapy outcome study. Responses indicated that 194 such studies were conducted. When the treatment findings were positive, 83% of the studies were submitted for publication. When the findings were negative, 43% of the investigations were submitted. Of the positive outcome studies, 74% were accepted for publication. Of the negative outcome studies, 50% were published. Thus, 61% of positive outcome studies were submitted *and* published, whereas 22% of negative outcome studies were submitted *and* published. Similarly, 61% of authors of published studies ($N = 68$) agreed with the statement, "If the research outcome is *not* statistically significant, there is little likelihood of the manuscript being published" (Kupfersmid & Fiala, 1991, p. 249).

Atkinson, Furlong, and Wampold (1982) studied the problem of whether manuscripts are differentially accepted or rejected primarily on the basis of statistical significance being reached with quality of experimental design and number of subjects held constant. Subjects were reviewers of two psychology journals ($N = 50$) who judged a manuscript in which only the Results section was altered to show either (a) a statistically significant outcome, (b) an outcome that *approached* statistical significance, or (c) results that were not statistically significant. When the paper reported statistically significant findings, 82% of the reviewers recommended publication; for negative results, only 37% of reviewers recommended acceptance for publication.

The above studies suggest that bias against negative outcomes is prevalent in the behavioral sciences' publication system. The next set of studies, however, provide an estimate of the extent to which articles reporting negative outcomes are actually published.

Sterling (1959/1970) examined 294 articles from four psychology journals and found that less than 3% of the articles retained the null hypothesis. A few years later, Smart (1964) reported that approximately 9% of articles from the 1961–1962 issues of the same four journals Sterling studied published negative results. Approximately 30 years later, articles from these same four journals were examined and less than 5% of the studies retained the null hypothesis (Sterling & Jang, 1988). Similarly, Bozarth and Roberts' (1972) survey of published articles in three psychology journals revealed that 6% retained the null hypothesis. These results, taken together, suggest that approximately 3% to 9% of articles published in psychology journals are those that retain the null hypothesis.

Further support for this estimate comes from Sterling's (1959/1970) findings that of 100 randomly selected articles summarized in *Psychological Abstracts*, approximately 5% reported negative outcomes. Smart (1964) followed up over a 5-year period on dissertations in psychology listed in *Dissertation Abstracts International*. He found that 12 of 23 dissertations having positive findings were published in comparison with 2 of 14 dissertations reporting negative results.

Several studies have compared the results of published versus unpublished experimental outcomes in the same area. These findings are expressed with the use of an effect size (ES) statistic, which involves subtracting the absolute value of the mean of the experimental group from that of the control group and dividing the value by either sample's standard deviation. (Homogeneity of variance is assumed.) An ES transforms scores into standard deviation units. Smith (1980) compared published ES scores with ES scores of doctoral dissertations in 12 areas of psychology. In all 12 fields, published ES scores were higher than unpublished scores. Across all 12 areas, the average ES for published studies was 0.64 whereas the average ES for dissertations was 0.43. Thus, an ES bias of 0.33 exists. Greater discrepancies are associated with probability of publication.

Smith, Glass, and Miller (1980) contrasted the ES of published psychotherapy outcome studies with that of ES scores reported in doctoral dissertations. The average ES for published articles was 0.87, for dissertations the average ES was 0.66. Eaton (1984) requested data from 34 researchers studying sex differences in human motor activity. Twenty-five authors responded to Eaton's request. He reported that the average ES for published articles in human motor performance is 0.47, for unpublished studies the average ES is 0.35. Perhaps the most dramatic demonstration of how experimental findings appearing in print may be a distortion as the result of publication bias was presented by Smith (1980). She examined sex bias in psychotherapy studies and found that "the effect size from published studies was .22, demonstrating counselor bias against females. The effect size from unpublished studies was − .24, demonstrating counselor bias *in favor* of females" (p. 24).

The above findings are not limited to journals in the behavioral sciences. Of 456 articles published in medical journals, only 15% had negative outcomes (Sterling & Jang, 1988). Simes (1987) claimed that medical journals are unlikely to publish statistically nonsignificant findings and, thus, reviews of clinical trials are biased. He provided data to support this claim by examining the effectiveness of two forms of treatment for advanced ovarian cancer. One form of treatment is chemotherapy, a second form of treatment is use of an alkylating agent first. If the alkylating agent fails to produce a positive response in the patient, chemotherapy is employed. Registered clinical trials were selected from protocols included in the International Cancer Research Data Bank. The dependent variable was patient survival. For those registered studies that were published, there is a modest effect in favor of the use of chemotherapy, having a median survival improvement rate of 16%–19%. For pooled registered trials, including published and unpublished data, there is no clear survival advantage between the two forms of treatment.

Sommer (1987) surveyed members of the Society for Menstrual Cycle Research and contrasted outcomes of 73 published articles with 28 unpublished studies. The researcher found that 73% of the positive outcome findings were published, whereas 54% of the negative outcomes reached print. Somewhat mitigating the concern over this form of bias were the results of research by Chalmers et al. (1990). They found no difference in cohort studies based on summary reports of published and unpublished investigations located in The Oxford Database of Perinatal Trials.

Amir and Sharon (1991) argued that it is entirely appropriate to publish papers reporting negative findings if the hypothesis is related to a prediction of a recognized theory advanced and the prediction does not occur. Studies in which there is no convincing reason for a prediction to be made should not be published when negative findings occur. The editor of *The New England Journal of Medicine*, Marcia Angell (1989), agreed with Amir and Sharon's position and stated, "we have no policy against publishing well-done negative studies. Indeed, we feel a particular obligation to publish a negative study when it contradicts an earlier study we have published and is of a similar or superior quality" (p. 465).

Former editor of the *Journal of Personality and Social Psychology* Anthony Greenwald (1975) stated *"support for the null hypothesis must be regarded as a research outcome that is as acceptable as any other"* (p. 16). The opinion of the former editor of *Applied Psychology* most closely reflects our position: "Perhaps p values are like mosquitoes. They have an evolutionary niche somewhere and no amount of scratching, swatting, or spraying will dislodge them" (Campbell, 1982/1985, p. 330).[1] (We take it that Campbell's reference was to using p values in retaining or rejecting a null hypothesis.)

---

[1] Also of concern is the power of a statistic—the probability that a statistical test will yield a statistically significant (i.e., reach or exceed a preset alpha value) and/or meaningful (i.e., reach or exceed a preset ES) level (Cohen, 1988). In the typical study in psychology, there is less than a 50% chance that the experimenter will find a medium ES (i.e., $r = .40$, Cohen, 1988; Sedlmeier & Gigerenzer, 1989). Increasing statistical power in behavioral science research, which can be accomplished by increasing the sample size, or preselecting a less stringent alpha level or desired ES, is an area that requires editor/reviewer attention.

3 CAUSES OF DISSATISFACTION: REPLICATION BIAS AND FRAUD

Beyond the problems associated with significance testing and the insistence on the acceptance of studies that demonstrate the rejection of null hypotheses are the unwillingness of editors to publish replication studies and failure of the scientific community to address the problem of fraudulent research reports.

Replication Bias

Before discussing this form of bias it is necessary to examine the way in which replication is conceptualized. Rosenthal (1991b) contends that "replication" is a relative term because use of the same subjects in the same experimental situation can never be exactly repeated. The closest one can get to the repeating of an original experiment is to perform the same experimental procedures again with subjects similar to those in the original study (Smith, 1970). The credibility of the outcome of a replication study increases if the experimenter enacting the replication is not the same individual who initially performed the experiment. Confidence in the results of the original experiment is also enhanced if the researcher performing the replication does not share the views held by the original experimenter (Rosenthal, 1991b).

Replication of a study for the purpose of verifying a significance statement is, of course, subject to the same potential flaws as was the original study. Lykken (1968/1970) proposed that "the only real solution to the problem of corroborating [clinical] theories is that of *multiple corroboration . . .* [which should] compel the respect of the most critical reader or editor" (pp. 272–273). But a reasonably large N and even a relatively small departure from a stated parameter are apt to authenticate the error. With these caveats in mind, replication studies must be considered a valuable source of verification.

If replication research findings are not being published, disconfirmatory results of original experiments are not available. This bias, like the bias against reporting negative results, places a discipline in the position where it is logically impossible to confirm an experimental outcome and, due to journal editorial policy, impossible to refute it.

> If twenty studies testing the same hypothesis are executed, on the average, [and there is no real difference] one of them will attain the .05 level of significance by chance alone. If this study is published, a result that is a Type I error, and nothing more, will appear in a professional journal. Not only will this Type I error be published but editorial policy guarantees that this error will never be publicly exposed! Only by allowing publication of replications and failures to replicate will Type I errors in the literature be uncovered. (Walster & Cleary, 1970, p. 17)

Neher (1967) insisted that only through replication can the problem of "probability pyramiding" be corrected. He defined probability pyramiding as "the cumulative inflation of probability levels resulting from biased selection [of manuscripts] at several successive stages from analysis to publication" (p. 259).

Probability pyramiding is a three-part problem, of which all parts are a direct result of the biases discussed here. The first part of probability pyramiding involves the conducting of an investigation and the performing of many types of statistical significance testing on the data because journal editors insist such tests be performed. Next, the researcher only reports findings where a statistically significant outcome has occurred because journal editors are unlikely to publish negative results. Third, editors select for publication only those studies where statistically significant outcomes are reported. Neher claimed that few professionals appreciate that "probability pyramiding [is] one of a general class of research errors" (p. 259).

Amir and Sharon (1991) maintained that before an experimental result could be considered valid, the findings should be reproducible and generalizable. Both criteria involve a form of replication. Reproducibility involves obtaining results similar to those of the original study when experimental methods are applied to a comparable sample in a similar manner to that of the original. Generalizability is a function of observing the same results when the original experimental methods are applied to a somewhat different sample.

However, there are several hurdles to be overcome by an investigator interested in conducting replication research. One of the first problems is obtaining original data or information from the author. Amir and Sharon (1991) randomly selected 35 studies from four social psychology journals and selected six studies to replicate. The investigators reported that information contained in the majority of studies was not detailed enough to allow for adequate replication. There have been four published attempts to obtain original data from a principal researcher. The interval between time of article publication and request for data spanned from one month (Craig & Reese, 1973) to several years (Eaton, 1984; Wolins, 1962).

Wolins (1962) made the first attempt. He reported that of 37 requests only 9 authors complied. An amazing 21 respondents told Wolins their data were misplaced or lost within 3 years of the time of original publication. Eaton (1984) made a similar request to 45 authors of original studies and obtained compliance in 25 cases. Seventy-five percent of these studies were published within 2 years of the time that Eaton made his request. For Craig and Reese (1973) there was a compliance rate of 20 out of 53 requests. Page (1975, cited in Hedrick, Boruch, & Ross, 1978) reported that of 70 requests, 34 researchers complied. Thus, a total of 205 requests for data from authors of original studies have been made with a compliance rate reaching only 43%.

The situation appears even worse for those who attempt to obtain original data/information from studies funded by the federal government or other public agencies. The following is a summary of the problems encountered in this area (Hedrick, Boruch, & Ross, 1978):

1. Funding sources often do not keep the original data.
2. The data may be stored in a variety of locations.
3. There is no standard method for the way data are stored, reported, or classified.
4. Project directors of funded studies often change assignments and are difficult to locate.
5. The individual who holds the data may be reluctant to release

information if subjects' confidentiality is not adequately protected.

6. The original investigator may not release data for fear that other researchers might (a) find fault with some aspect of the experiment or its analysis and/or (b) make an important discovery based on examination of the data.

A second hurdle is the selection of the type of statistic to employ. Even if the replication study used the *exact* number of subjects under the exact experimental conditions, the odds are 50–50 that the replication study could result in a statistically significant outcome if a replicator employed statistical significance testing where p ≤ .05 (Humphreys, 1980).

Figure 1 illustrates how the 50–50 odds of a replication study finding statistical significance operate. As noted, the distribution of the experimental group overlaps 5% of the distribution of the control group scores. Should a one-tailed test of significance be used where $p \leq .05$, statistical significance is reached. If the experimental sample's distribution truly reflects the distribution in its population, and 100 replications were conducted, 50% of the sample means would fall to the left of the distribution of the experimental group depicted in Figure 1 and 50% of the sample means would fall to the right. Thus, one half of the replication studies would have a sample in which scores reached statistical significance, and one half of the replication sample's scores would not reach statistical significance.

Rosenthal (1991b) pointed out that if a published study reported a statistically significant difference utilizing 64 subjects, the statistical power of that study equals .50. With a statistical power of .50 there is only a 25% chance of the original and replication studies both resulting in a statistically significant outcome at $p \leq .05$. He suggested that an effect size (ES) statistic be employed to determine if agreement/non-agreement between two studies exists. The product of this statistical procedure may be interpreted in two ways. One method is to construct a 95% confidence interval around the ES obtained in the original study and the ES obtained in the replication. If the confidence intervals overlap, no difference is assumed between the original and replication samples and agreement has been reached.

A second method involves establishing guidelines as to what is considered a "weak" through a "strong" range of difference in terms of ES scores. Most researchers have adopted Cohen's (1988) rule of thumb

Figure 1
Hypothetical Sample Distribution for an Original Study

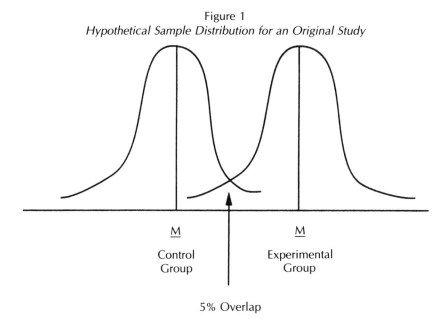

M	M
Control Group	Experimental Group

5% Overlap

that an ES of .2 is a small effect, .5 a medium effect, and .8 or higher a large effect. In replication research, if the ES between the original and replicated samples is .2 or less, little difference is assumed to exist and the results of the original study are supported (Wolf, 1986).

To compare correlation coefficients, Humphreys (1980) advised researchers *not* to compare the rs in the original and replication research with the hypothetical population value of zero. Rather, the rs between the two studies should be compared directly with each other by transforming each r into its corresponding Fisher z value and dividing the difference by the standard error. This, in effect, creates a t score and a t table is consulted to determine if there is a statistically significant difference between the two coefficients. (See Cohen, 1988; Rosenthal, 1991a, 1991b, for other appropriate procedures.)

After determining the most appropriate statistical method for comparing the results of a replication study with that of an original, the researcher is faced with a third hurdle. Bornstein (1991b) pointed out that an experimenter undertaking replication research is in a paradoxical situation. If the original outcome is supported, journal editors may find the study trivial. If the study fails to support the original, the replication research is reporting statistically nonsignificant results.

> There is a vague sense of disrespect for someone who is interested in doing replications. Prime journals will reject it, usually with an explanation that the paper is not a contribution to new knowledge. Replications are often second-class citizens in the social science literature. (Hendrick, 1991, p. 42)

Rosenthal (1991b) noted that when a replication study's outcome does not support the findings of the original investigation it is difficult to determine which of the two studies is more accurate. To mitigate this dilemma, Rosenthal suggested that two replications be conducted. The first replication should be done in a manner very similar to that of the original; the second should be moderately dissimilar. If the ES in the first replication is not significantly different from that of the original, support has been provided. If the ES in the second replication is significantly different from the original, the original findings are interpreted to be limited in external validity/generalizability.

The last hurdle that scientists performing replication research face is the bias against actual publication of their papers. Thirty-four percent of peer reviewers from three Canadian journals stated they would be very likely to recommend rejection of any replication study submitted (Rowney & Zenisek, 1980). Seventy-one percent of editors and reviewers of management journals also claimed they would reject a replication study for publication (Kerr et al., 1977). These attitudes are also reflected in studies examining the percentage of replicated research published in the literature.

Sterling (1959/1970) found that less than 1% of the 362 articles published in four psychology journals were replications. Bozarth and Roberts (1972) reported that less than 1% of 1,334 articles published in three psychology journals were replications. Similarly, of 100 randomly selected summaries of articles described in *Psychological Abstracts*, only one was a replication (Sterling, 1959/1970). Sterling and Jang (1988) repeated Sterling's (1959/1970) study utilizing the same four psychology journals 30 years later. Of the 597 articles published, 6% were replications. When three medical journals involving 456 articles were examined, less than 1% of the studies were replications.

Reid, Soley, and Wimmer (1981; cited in Armstrong, 1982) reported that of 30 replications of published studies in advertising journals, 12 failed to support the original results. Wong (1981) stated:

> I must make the painful disclosure that in the past few years, in numerous experiments, I have failed to replicate some of the

widely accepted findings enshrined in psychology textbooks and have also learned of several other investigators with similar experiences. (p. 690)

It is not clear what type of statistical analysis these replication researchers employed. It is unlikely that any of these studies would be submitted for publication given the current bias against publishing such endeavors. Thus, a critical evaluation of the credibility of the original studies cannot be made because replication studies are rarely published. Likewise, the credibility of those stating they have failed to replicate cannot be judged because these studies will not be submitted for publication, and if submitted, will not be published.

In spite of the critical importance replication plays in helping to differentiate credible from noncredible findings, the bias against publishing such studies is considerable. However, Hunt (1975) argued that replication research is going on continually. He stated that the essential characteristic of a replication study is the particular hypothesis being tested, especially the hypothesis' ability to predict some relevant outcome: "Therefore, as long as we replicate hypotheses, we need not worry about additional replications" (p. 589). For Hunt, it is not critical that a replication match the original in experimental method, sample selected, or the way in which independent or dependent variables are conceptualized or measured. He appeared to believe that a literature review on a topic (a hypothesis) is a form of replication analysis.

What Hunt did not adequately detail is how to judge what are to be considered disconfirmatory results. There have, for example, been many literature reviews on the effectiveness of psychotherapy. The general hypothesis tested is the degree to which psychotherapy has a positive effect on mental health. If one study investigated the benefits of psychoanalysis on children in play therapy and another study examined the effects of behavior therapy on reducing phobias in adults, it is hard to determine what Hunt would conclude if the first study reported a positive result and the second study did not. Yet, both studies could be conceptualized as investigating the same general hypothesis.

Who but Hunt would believe that the second study disconfirmed the findings of the first? His approach not only appears extremely questionable (or requires greater clarification), but seems to confuse the external validity (generalization of the findings) issue with that of replication. Additionally, if Hunt's position had merit, there would be little need in experimental studies for a detailed Methods section, because the hypothesis being tested would be the critical factor and not the procedures used or the sample employed.

The Quantity/Quality Problem

Although the exact figure is not known, it is probable that a large number of scientists must publish to be hired and/or promoted. A national survey of university faculty initiated by the Carnegie Foundation for the Advancement of Teaching found that 77% of respondents agreed with the statement: "In my department it is difficult for a person to achieve tenure if he or she does not publish." For this same sample 80% answered that it was "very important" or "fairly important" to the question: "How important is the number of publications for granting tenure in your department?" (Boyer, 1990). As a result, the quantity of papers in print assumes priority over all else.

The publish or perish policy of many institutions promotes the quantity over quality phenomenon of which many researchers are often captive employees. When it comes to job security and promotion "one is always tempted to count the number of publications—anything but read them" (Ghislen, 1989, p. 71). Broad (1981) stated that it is a practice of many scientists to write papers for journal submission that are the "Least Publishable Unit" (LPU). The practice of LPU involves conducting one experiment, performing many statistical analyses on a variety of hypotheses, and publishing as many articles as possible based on this one study. Typically, the experimenter submits several papers for publication, each testing one or two hypotheses. If he or she can appear to legitimately test 10 hypotheses from one study, several potential publications are possible. One study that generates five 3-page articles provides greater job security than one 15-page (or, for that matter, 50-page) study in print.

In addition to the creation of a great number of articles having negligible worth, the current dynamics surrounding the professional publication process promote a "play it safe" formula. Nisbett (1978), a prominent social psychologist, advised behavioral scientists interested in increasing the probability of publishing their studies to avoid creative or innovative designs and to concentrate efforts on areas that are easy to test and are noncontroversial. Finke (1990), writing in the *American Psychologist*, believes Nisbett's "advice" is fastidiously followed by many psychologists. "Research that is readily published tends to be excessively conventional and platitudinous, whereas studies that are highly original and that constitute innovative advances in the field often are rejected because the reviewers are uninformed, quixotic, or simply irresponsible" (p. 669).

Sociologist Duncan Lindsey (1978) agreed with such conclusions: "The critical, the controversial, the imaginative are not allowed to see the light of day. To the extent that the professional journals do not encourage controversial work, the spirit of science has been diminished" (p. 120). Ghiselin (1989), a comparative anatomist, stated that "the [publication] system mitigates against creativity, initiative, and even candor" (p. 67). He concluded:

> If somebody's work is unusual, it will be hard to evaluate by any standard. If it is controversial, there will never be a consensus. . . . What academia really wants is a product that sells and gets no complaints from the customers. Instead of real creativity it is apt to promote mere "trendiness." (p. 71)

Fraud

The current motivation for many to publish, coupled with the three noted biases of editors, engenders considerable conventionality where monotony prevails and science progresses less than optimally. The present system also creates the opportunity for the existence of undetected fraud. The publish or perish policy co-existing with the bias against publishing statistically nonsignificant findings supports a climate where a continuum of data distortion is likely to occur. Because negative outcome and replication studies rarely reach print, detection of questionable data is probably infrequent. The issue of fraud is contentious and, thus, requires greater explication.

Writing for the *APA Monitor*, Adler (1991) listed 21 fraudulent behaviors that a researcher might exhibit. These behaviors are listed in Table 1. The focus of this discussion is on what are considered the two most serious forms of fraud, data fabrication and data altering. Broad and Wade (1982b) claimed that examination of fraudulent behavior in scientists provides a window into how science operates:

> Cases of fraud provide telling evidence not just about how well the checking system of science works in practice, but also about the fundamental nature of science—about the scientific method,

Table 1
Adler's (1991) List of Scientific Fraudulent Behavior

Data fabrication	Undisclosed repetition of study
Data falsification	Selective reporting of findings
Plagiarism	Failure to publish
Unethical treatment of subjects	Refusal to share data
Undisclosed conflicts of interest	Inappropriate statistical tests
Violation of privileged material	Misleading reporting
Irresponsible authorship credit	Redundant publication
Failure to retain data	Fragmentary publication
Inadequate supervision of study	Inappropriate citations
Sloppy recording of data	Intentional sloppy manuscript
Data-dredging	

about the relation of fact to theory, about the motives and attitudes of scientists. (p. 8)

Sechrest (1987) outlined a variety of conditions that are apt to encourage fraudulent actions:

1. Scientists have no formal ethical training and are often exploited by senior researchers during graduate training.
2. For some scientists, securing funding and obtaining salary increases, awards, and promotions are often contingent on the outcome of research projects.
3. An experimenter is rarely asked to provide the original data. If such a request is made, there is no negative consequence for those who refuse outright.
4. Because economic survival and/or status may hinge on achieving a statistically significant outcome, a little "fudging" of data can determine whether a p value exceeded the rejection level.
5. The probability of getting caught for cheating is very low.

In addition to conditions existing that may engender a favorable climate for cheating, there are several dynamics operating at the institutional level that contribute to the problem. Nobel (1990) asked the deans of all accredited medical schools in the United States ($N = 133$)

questions regarding procedures that they employ to help to ensure that research is being conducted in a nonfraudulent manner at their school. Only 17 claimed to have any written procedures at all in this area and only 9 of them forwarded their guidelines to Nobel.

Fisher (1982) reported in the *APA Monitor* that universities are reluctant to probe for potential fraud because they may find it. Grants are usually awarded to agencies, not to individual scientists. If fraud is uncovered, it is on the institution that responsibility falls. This, of course, reduces the facility's chance of receiving future grant funds. Similarly, because most published articles include the author's name and affiliation, the credibility of all researchers associated with an institution is damaged when fraud is detected. Adler (1991) stated that "university administrators still feel pressure to overlook cases of fraud, especially if the person is bringing in a lot of grant money" (p. 11).

When APA members' opinions were sought ($N = 76$) regarding the nature of sanctions that should be imposed on researchers who fabricated data or plagiarized, "plagiarism was rated as warranting formal university action more than fabrication of data" (Riordan & Marlin, 1987, p. 106). This is an incredible finding! Psychologists apparently believe that it is more serious for a scientist to take credit for another's writing than to purposely distort data. When plagiarism occurs neither the accumulation of knowledge nor its accuracy is negatively influenced. What occurs is potential miscredit for a statement. However, falsified data can lead to misguided support for a theory and/or improper treatment. The greater penalty recommended for the plagiarizer than the data fabricator suggests that behavioral scientists are often more attuned to the assignment of credit—to the protection of the "rights" of an author—than to the formulation of an accurate data base. If this conclusion is tenable, those who believe many publications are written primarily for the authors' advancement, rather than for the advancement of knowledge, have further support.

Examples of how fraudulent data have influenced theories in the behavioral sciences and, thus, what is believed to be valid about human behavior are illustrated in the cases of Cyril Burt, J. B. Watson, and Stephen Breuning. The data presented by all three individuals had a significant impact on what professionals believed—and did—about a number of aspects of human functioning.

The extent to which an individual is capable of learning is believed to be reflected in scores on standardized measures of intellectual functioning. For over a century the nature-nurture debate regarding the degree to which intelligence is primarily biologically fixed (nature) versus the position that intelligence is greatly modifiable by enriched environments (nurture) has been argued. It is widely acknowledged that the capacity for learning is influenced by both biological and environmental conditions. The *degree* to which learning can be influenced by the environment has been the point of contention.

If the hereditarians are correct and approximately 80% of the spread of scores on a test of intelligence are attributable to biological endowment, some have argued (incorrectly) that educational programs will have little success in increasing the knowledge and skills of those children who function in the lower and middle ranges of intelligence. If the environmentalists are correct, large expenditures for the investigation of a variety of educational programs' effectiveness are warranted.

But which position is more tenable? Behavioral scientists recognize that the best means of evaluating the influence of genetic effects versus those of the environment in determining intellectual functioning is through the study of monozygotic (MZ) twins (identical twins having the exact same genetic make up) who are reared in different environments when compared to those reared in the same environment. Obtaining a sample of such twins is not easy. However, in three studies, spanning the period 1955 through 1966, Cyril Burt published research specifically addressing this issue.

Considerable suspicion surrounds these articles, including the existence of an author and co-author. Margaret Howard is listed as Burt's co-author for one of the studies and J. Conway is listed as the lone author of another. However, no one has been able to locate either of these ladies. Burt's secretary, in one instance, reported that Burt actually authored the J. Conway article. (He was prone to occasionally using a pseudonym.) However, in another instance, "Burt's secretary testified that he had told her that Conway had emigrated, perhaps to Australia" (Jensen, 1992, p. 117).

Burt's data were considered the best test of the nature *vs.* nurture argument because he claimed to have secured the largest known sample of MZ twins reared apart soon after birth. In 1955 Burt reported data on 21 sets of MZ twins reared apart. In 1958 he presented data on over 30 such sets of twins, and in 1965 his sample had grown to 53 MZ twin pairs reared apart. Additionally, in those three studies the sample of MZ twin pairs reared together increased from an N of 83 to an N of 95. For MZ twins reared apart, the average correlation between the intellectual functioning of each twin pair was reported to be $r = .771$;

for MZ twins reared together the average r = .944 (Kamin, 1974). Based on these data, it was assumed that intellectual functioning is mainly attributable to genetic endowment.

However, all this changed with Leon Kamin's (1974) book *The Science and Politics of I.Q.* Kamin's investigation convincingly demonstrated that (a) the exact nature of the IQ tests employed by Burt is actually unknown, (b) how scores were derived remains ambiguous, (c) there are no raw data available on any of Burt's subjects, and (d) the evidence that MZ twin pairs were raised in different environments is questionable. Kamin reported that many twin pairs were raised by relatives or foster families whose social class (believed to be a rough measure of environment) was similar. But, the astounding thing was that Kamin recognized the obvious—the correlation for MZ twins reared separately in all three studies, regardless of changing sample N, remained exactly at r = .771. This is incredible statistical stability! Likewise, in all three studies the correlation for MZ twins reared together did not depart from r = .994. Kamin (1974) concluded:

> The absence of procedural description in Burt's reports vitiates their scientific utility. The frequent arithmetical inconsistencies and mutually contradictory descriptions cast doubt upon the entire body of his later work. The marvelous consistency of his data supporting the hereditarian position often taxes credibility; and on analysis, the data are found to contain implausible effects consistent with an effort to prove the hereditarian case. The conclusion cannot be avoided: The numbers left behind by Professor Burt are simply not worthy of our current scientific attention. (p. 47)

J. B. Watson was the consummate environmentalist to the degree that Burt was an exemplar hereditarian. Watson held that through the principles of classical conditioning, behaviors and emotions are learned. He believed there are three innate (unlearned) emotional states: fear, rage, and love. He argued that as a result of classical conditioning, a great range of stimuli can evoke these three emotions.

Watson's classic demonstration was his study on conditioned fear in a child, little Albert (Watson & Rayner, 1920). In this study a loud noise was paired with Albert's petting of a rat. Watson's goal was to transfer little Albert's natural fear of loud noises (unconditioned response) to fearfulness of rats' fur (conditioned response) and to have this fear generalize to many furry-like objects, including a rabbit, a dog, the beard on a Santa Claus mask, and human hair. However, there is evidence that loud noises did not ever result in fearfulness.

In one of Watson's accounts of the experiment, he noted that when distraught, Albert would put his thumb in his mouth. When this occurred, attempts at eliciting a fearful reaction were not possible. Furthermore, a movie was made of the little Albert experiment. The film captures an individual removing Albert's thumb from his mouth. Thus, the whole issue of whether loud noises produced an unlearned fearful reaction in Albert (much less whether this emotional reaction was generalized to other stimuli) is questionable. Additionally, attempts at replicating the experiment failed. Samelson (1980) concluded that Watson's "procedure raises all kinds of questions about the experimental techniques used and even more questions about the selectivity of the published protocol" (p. 621).

For the last 20 years stimulant medications, such as Ritalin® and Cylert®, have been used to help children exhibiting disorders of attention and/or hyperactivity. Breuning published a series of studies in which he reported that stimulants have a positive effect on reducing hyperactivity in large numbers of children with mental retardation. He claimed to have tested the effectiveness of stimulants against that of other psychotropic medications in hundreds of mentally retarded youth. If his studies were valid, it would be legitimate to recommend that these medications be used to reduce the overactivity level of many mentally retarded youngsters. However, his results were questioned by several researchers. An investigation by the National Institute of Mental Health (NIMH), which funded some of Breuning's work, was initiated. The NIMH inquiry found that there was no evidence that Breuning conducted the studies he claimed. He was prosecuted and convicted of scientific fraud in federal court (Garfield & Welljams-Dorof, 1990).

An obvious question is: How prevalent is scientific fraud? It is difficult to determine if the three cited examples in this text are representative of an undercurrent of deceit and data fabrication or simply illustrate a dramatic anomaly in the history of science. Unfortunately, the extent to which fraud exists in science is one of the least explored areas. Part of the reason for this lack of concern by the scientific community is that there is an erroneous belief that science polices itself via the peer review process and replication research (Broad & Wade, 1982b).

In this chapter we have demonstrated how replication cannot detect data fraud because editors are biased against publishing such studies. As a result, experimenters are unlikely to conduct replications. The feebleness of the peer review system to detect data fabrication and other forms of fraud is exemplified in the three examples given as well as in a number of fraudulent cases reviewed by Broad and Wade (1982b). In the majority of cases, colleagues working in the same facility or laboratory were most often responsible for discovering the deception.

Rosenthal (1978) investigated the misrecording of raw data (what was seen or heard) in 21 studies. He reported that errors were made in 1% of the recordings. Of these errors, two thirds were errors made in the direction that supported the research hypothesis. A 1% error rate may not seem like a great deal of data contamination. However, this form of distortion is probably only the tip of the iceberg. An investigation by the Food and Drug Administration found that of 50 studies audited, 32% contained falsified data (Broad & Wade, 1982a). The sheer number of recent articles appearing in the *APA Monitor* addressing the issue of dishonesty in behavioral science research attests to the increasing concern regarding the issue (Adler, 1989, 1991; Fisher, 1982; Hostetler, 1987a, 1987b, 1987c, 1987d).

Another topic that has received little attention is the process by which researchers in a field are informed that fraudulent data exist. Once counterfeit data are discovered it is important to communicate this to the scientific community and to remove the influence these data may have on the field. Thus far, only two studies have addressed that issue. Both studies involve fraudulent data published in biomedical journals.

Pfeifer and Snodgrass (1990) investigated the effect that a retraction of data has on citation rates of those affected articles. The authors identified 82 articles summarized in the *Medical Index* in which retractions were published. Articles published in the same journal during the same year as each retracted article served as a control group. They followed the citation rates for both retracted and control groups' articles for the first nine years after each article was published/retracted. The investigators reported that retraction of an article reduced its citation frequency by approximately 35% in comparison with nonretracted controls during the same time interval. There was no indication that obscure and/or non-high status journal articles cited retracted papers in greater proportions than papers published in more highly recognized journals.

Friedman (1990) studied the behavior of editors of 30 biomedical journals involving 135 publications by Robert Slutsky, whose research was found to be fraudulent. Slutsky was a medical researcher who published in journals focusing on cardiology, nuclear medicine, and radiology (Engler, Covell, Friedman, Kitcher, & Peters, 1987). Slutsky's attorney sent letters retracting 15 of Slutsky's articles to the eight journals that published them. Six of these journals printed a retraction. For the 135 articles published by Slutsky in 30 journals, 18 have published a statement questioning the validity of 64 of the articles. Eight journals elected not to publish any retraction. The editors of all 30 journals were contacted, 15 of whom replied. Of these, 14 stated their journal has no written retraction policy.

The few studies conducted in this area suggest that even written public acknowledgment that data have been falsified is unlikely to be greatly circulated among the community of scientists. Some journals refuse to print retractions outright. Even when retractions are printed, Pfeifer and Snodgrass' (1990) findings on citations suggest that the majority of investigators are probably not aware of data misrepresentation when it becomes public.

The current situations governing the backdrop against which professional publications in the behavioral sciences operate are:

1. Many behavioral scientists' jobs, promotions, and reputations hinge on the *quantity* of their publications.

2. Low-risk studies are often selected for investigation because of the higher probability of meeting editor/reviewer criteria for publishability.

3. Editors'/reviewers' bias for statistical significance testing as the preferred means of hypothesis testing, coupled with the bias toward publishing those studies reporting a statistically significant outcome almost exclusively, guarantees Type I error and other built-in data contaminants.

4. For an unknown percentage of investigators, the pressure to publish creates an atmosphere that ranges from selective reporting of data to that of data fraud.

5. Due to the editor/reviewer bias against publishing negative results and/or replication studies, it is very difficult to evaluate effectively which experimental results have credibility and which results are spurious.

Unfortunately for the scientific community, as well as for society at large, there is no forum, no authority, no one person or institution that is in a position to do more than express distress about such practices. With this text, we are appealing to researchers, journal editors, and reviewers. Perhaps we should appeal to the APA, which is recognized as a leading organization in the field of research literature. Unless some firm stand is taken somewhere, it is probably futile to expect the thousands of researchers, teachers of research, and perhaps even consumers of such data to change their practices in spite of their impact on the quality of data being published.

4 WRITING BETTER ARTICLES

The preceding two chapters have a pessimistic flavor. Behavioral scientists as well as professionals in other fields bemoan the fact that the quality of professional publications is poor, the motivation to publish is often ego-centered rather than knowledge-driven, and the biases exercised by journal editors make it difficult to refute outcomes that have been published. However, it is our conviction that quality studies can become part of the literature if both authors and editors modify some of their current practices.

The purpose of this chapter is to provide specific recommendations, made by ourselves as well as others, that we believe will enhance the quality of a paper. Guidelines on the selection of significant problems to study and recommendations for the use of meaningful statistical analysis will be discussed. Additionally, information about the publication process and the peer review system will be provided. The better one's understanding of the publication process, the more likely pitfalls of publishing only what is easy may be avoided; and the less likely one may become discouraged with the entire publication enterprise and abandon research altogether.

Focus on Significant Issues

The fundamental rule for producing quality studies is to focus on consequential questions. "Outstanding scientists . . . discriminate between work that is worth publishing and that which . . . is best left unpublished though it could easily find its way into print" (Merton, 1963/ 1973, p. 455). The result of Merton's (1963/1973) interviews with Nobel Laureates is informative. The respondents pointed out that it is more important to examine *what* to study rather than to spend large amounts of time contemplating *how* to study a phenomenon.

> Almost invariably they [Nobel Laureates] lay great emphasis on the importance of problem-*finding*, not only problem-solving. They uniformly express the strong conviction that what matters most in their work is a developing sense of taste, of judgment, in seizing upon problems that are of fundamental importance. (p. 453)

Other behavioral scientists have stressed the nature of the topic or research problem addressed as critical to producing important findings. When editors of psychology journals ($N = 66$) were asked to rank order 15 characteristics that make for a quality article, "contribution to knowledge" placed at the top of this list (Wolff, 1973) (in spite of the fact that they accepted articles for publication principally on the issue of whether the null hypothesis was rejected!). Similarly, the editor for the *Academy of Management* analysis of 1,005 manuscripts submitted to that journal concluded that the importance of the topic studied and the appropriateness of the topic emerged as two of the three most frequent factors associated with papers judged as publishable (Cummings, Frost, & Vakil, 1985).

An obvious concern for some researchers is how to identify important topics. Each specialization has its own set of important questions. If one is new to a particular specialty, reading salient literature review articles is a good place to locate relevant topics. In formulating an experimental or quasi-experimental study, the relevance of an investigation can often be assessed by asking questions regarding the interpretation of the three possible outcomes, using procedures required by reviewers and publishers. For most studies these are:

1. There is a statistically significant difference between the experimental and control group and this difference is large (meaningful), or the correlation (which also includes multiple regression, factor analysis) between the independent variable(s) and dependent variable(s) is statistically significant and the accounted-for variance is considerable.

2. There is a statistically significant difference between the experimental and control group, but this difference is slight, or the correlation between the independent variable(s) and dependent variable(s) is statistically significant but only a small amount of variance is accounted for.

3. There is a trivial difference between experimental and control groups, or there is very little accounted-for variance between the independent and dependent variable(s).

If an investigator can adequately answer the question of what action may follow on each of these outcomes to himself or herself and to his or her colleagues' satisfaction regardless of which of the three above outcomes occurs, he or she can be relatively confident that the study has relevance. This is especially true if one's colleagues appreciate the importance of the study even if the experimental outcome is that of the last example above. Like a good survey study, if the investigator has selected a representative sample, has asked important questions, and receives a high return rate, then the actual percentages of respondents answering "yes" vs. "no" on each question are not important. Regardless of the outcome (percentages of "yes" vs. "no" for each question), the results are apt to be highly informative.

Support for the above guidelines comes from several sources. Former editor of the *Journal of Personality and Social Psychology* Anthony Greenwald (1976) contended that a paper has quality if "the results of the reported research could have been interesting if they had come out differently from those reported" (p. 41). The editor of *The New England Journal of Medicine* commented that "when a good study addresses an important question, the answer is interesting and the work deserves publication, whether the result is positive or negative" (Angell, 1989, pp. 465–466).

Mahoney (1976) reminded scientists that research efforts attending to important problems are publishable as long as acceptable research designs are used. If a psychoanalyst was interested in convincing the editor of a behavioristically oriented journal to publish a study demonstrating that the use of reinforcement is irrelevant to the successful treatment of some disorder, the psychoanalyst would have to provide supporting data that were generated from a research design considered valid by behaviorists (perhaps a within-subjects ABAB design).

Similarly, Wolff's (1973) sample of journal editors rated the adequacy of an investigator's research design as the second most critical characteristic in determining the quality of a study. The editor of *Academy of Management* also included the competency of the research design as one of three prime factors contributing to a paper's acceptance for publication (Cummings et al., 1985). It is also important to have reliable and valid measures of each variable and a clear and convincing rationale for each measure selected (Campbell, 1982/1985; Maher, 1978).

The third characteristic contributing to a quality study is inclusion of a representative sample of subjects (Campbell, 1982/1985; Maher, 1978). Psychotherapists give little credence to studies where college students or individuals responding to newspaper advertisements are used as subjects to "test" some clinical technique (Barlow, Hays, & Nelson, 1984). Korn and Bram (1988) reviewed sample selection in three social psychology journals. They reported that 83% of all studies ($N = 197$) used college students as subjects. Too many experiments conducted in the behavioral sciences include subjects not representative of the population they are assumed to depict. Often, the subjects selected for study are those that are most readily available—and compliant.

Overcoming the Problem of Statistical Significance Testing

It is clear that in most instances only those experimental studies that report statistically significant findings are published. Not only does this procedure cause Type I errors to proliferate and encourage data selection bias and outright fraud, but the very practice of conducting tests of statistical significance as a method of information interpretation is itself highly debatable.

In Chapter Two, we stated our contention that conducting a test of statistical significance is an inappropriate aspect of data analysis. Unfortunately, it is often the first *and last* step an author undertakes. This view is widely accepted. Meehl (1978), for example, challenged the usefulness of significance testing as an element in the decision-making process: "*it is always more valuable to show approximate agreement of observations with a theoretically predicted numerical point value, rank order, or function form, than it is to compute a 'precise probability' that something merely differs from something else*" (p. 825).

A variety of alternatives to statistical significance testing have been suggested. The three most frequently mentioned are (a) confidence intervals, (b) correlation ratios or other degree of accounted-for variance measures (R^2), and (c) effect size.

A researcher of the early literature in the behavioral sciences revealed that the use of a confidence interval, in the form of a Probability Error (PE), was the most popular method of data presentation (Tversky & Kahneman, 1971). The PE is a 50% confidence interval constructed around a mean score. If a group has a mean score of 30 with a PE of 5, there is a 50% chance the true score for this population is between 25 through 35.

In the 1920s, when Fisher began publishing his books on statistics, 3PE (three times the Probability Error) was frequently used for determining statistical significance in many areas of science. Similarly, 3PE was employed as a criterion determining "significance" when the t test was developed (Cowles & Davis, 1982).

> Although, strictly speaking, the conventional rejection level of 3PE is equivalent to two times the SD (in modern terminology, a z score of 2), which expressed as a percentage is about 4.56%, one may hazard a guess that Fisher simply rounded off this value to 5% for ease of explanation. (Cowles & Davis, 1982, p. 557)

Many statistics texts discuss the value of confidence intervals, but journal editors have not promoted their use. "The usual reason for constructing a confidence interval is to obtain a range of values such that a set proportion (called a *confidence level*, or *level of confidence*) of such intervals over the long run would contain the true population parameter" (Henkel, 1976, p. 73). Typically, a 95% confidence interval is constructed, but this range is arbitrary. It appears the only reason a 95% confidence interval is utilized is because this confidence level range is tied to statistical significance testing when $p \leq .05$. If null hypothesis testing is operative, a researcher can reject the null if the range of scores within the 95% confidence interval does not include the value of zero.

Cohen (1990) recommended that an 80% confidence interval be considered in some instances. As is the case with alpha levels, no predetermined confidence interval can be specified as being "correct." It is recommended that all confidence intervals measured be reported, as well as percent of overlap between experimental and control groups.

The use of confidence intervals allows scientists the potential for estimating a parameter's value. As studies accumulate in a given area, as experimental procedures improve, and as different samples are measured, the accuracy of parameter estimation increases. Behavioral scientists are much better informed when they know the value (or precise range of values) of a variable as opposed to simply knowing whether a variable has a nonzero value. Hoaglin and Andrews (1975) as well as Salsburg (1985) have recommended that biomedical journals replace p values with confidence interval estimations.

The correlation ratio and/or the squared value of a correlation coefficient, termed the coefficient of determination (R^2), provide researchers with a value estimate of the degree to which knowledge of one variable (or a combination of variables, e.g., multiple regression, canonical correlation) accounts for the spread of scores in another variable(s). As the value of the correlation ratio or coefficient of determination increases, the degree of prediction becomes more precise.

The correlation ratio or coefficient of determination expresses the magnitude of a relationship, rather than being simply a measure of a nonzero relationship. Thus, when a theory predicts a relationship among variables and this is supported empirically, an incentive is provided for researchers to perform experimental manipulations of the independent variables. Even though the cost of performing such research is high (and it is understood that correlational studies do not imply causal relationships between variables), there is reason to be optimistic about discovering valuable information.

Correlation ratios and coefficients of determination, like confidence intervals, can also be compared across a wide variety of studies assessing the same phenomenon. As changes in the degree of experimental control and the nature of the sample employed are evaluated across an array of studies, the degree of change in the magnitude of the relationship that occurs between independent variable(s) with that of the dependent variable(s) can be determined. Another advantage of using accounted-for variance as a measure of experimental effect is that t tests, F tests, chi square, and effect size statistics can all be transformed into correlation coefficients (Wolf, 1986).

With respect to correlational research, Rosenthal (1991a) suggested that to determine whether a significant difference has occurred, the rs in the original and replication studies should be transformed to Fisher z scores. The respective z scores should be subtracted with a confidence interval being constructed around the difference. If the confidence interval includes a zero value, the replicated results agree with the original findings—there is no difference between the correlations in the two studies. Rosenthal also recommended that Cohen's q be used to determine whether a significant difference between the ES of the two correlation coefficients has been reached (see Cohen, 1988; Rosenthal, 1991a). Again, arbitrary guidelines have been constructed. An $r = .10$ is considered a small effect; $r = .30$ a medium effect; and $r = .50$ or higher a large effect (Wolf, 1986).

Rosenthal and Rubin (1982) promoted the use of R^2 in the form of a binomial effect size display (BESD). The BESD provides a value that addresses the question "What is the effect on the success rate (e.g., survival rate, cure rate, improvement rate, selection rate, etc.) of the institution of a certain treatment procedure?" (p. 166). The authors presented BESD tables that convert correlation coefficients into differential success rates. They demonstrated that an $r = .10$ converts into a 10% difference in ratio of success; an $r = .20$ transforms into a 20% difference in success rate, etc. They illustrated how the BESD table works by providing an example from psychotherapy research.

Smith and Glass (1977, cited in Rosenthal & Rubin, 1982) performed a meta-analysis literature review on over 400 psychotherapy outcome studies. Their results (reported in effect size) transform into a correlation coefficient such that psychotherapy accounts for approximately 10% of the improvement variance ($r = .32$, $R^2 = .10$) over nonpsychotherapy controls. Rosenthal and Rubin demonstrated that such results suggest that 66% of those in psychotherapy treatment improved compared to 34% improvement for the controls, commenting that this is not a trivial difference.

Rosenthal (1990) provided an example in which a seemingly small correlation can indicate an important treatment effect. He reported that a randomized double blind study addressing the potential of aspirin to reduce heart attacks was terminated because the data clearly indicated that aspirin does reduce the risk of future heart attacks by approximately 4%. This finding was based on data where $r = .034$. "The conclusion that [a] treatment is unimportant because it accounts for only [a small percent] of the variance is simply wrong. Percent of variance explained can, in some cases, then, be a very deceptive measure" (Rosenthal & Rubin, 1979, p. 395).

Perhaps making the greatest gains in popularity as a form of statistical analysis is the use of effect size (ES or Cohen's d). ES is becoming the statistic of choice for those conducting literature reviews, especially in the form of meta-analysis. As noted in Chapter Two, ES involves subtracting the absolute value of the mean of the experimental group from that of the control group and dividing the product by the standard deviation (either the standard deviation of the experimental or control group may be used because homogeneity of variance is assumed). In essence, ES transforms all scores into standard deviation units. ES is a measure of magnitude expressed in standard deviation units to which a phenomenon is present in a population (Cohen, 1988).

> It can now readily be made clear that when the null hypothesis is false, it is false to some specific degree, i.e., *the effect size (ES) is some specific nonzero value in the population.* The larger this value, the greater the *degree* to which the phenomenon under study is manifested. (Cohen, 1988, p. 10)

Additionally, *t* tests, F tests, and correlation coefficients can all be transformed into ES values (Wolf, 1986). The editor of *Measurement and Evaluation in Counseling and Development* (Thompson, 1988) formally recommended the regular use of ES as the statistic of choice. Similarly, Houglin and Andrews (1975) advised biomedical journals to dispense with *p* values and replace them with ES (and confidence intervals) statistics.

The use of confidence intervals, degree of accounted-for variance, and ES presents methods of statistical analysis that, when coupled with selection of an important topic, use of suitable research designs, and the inclusion of a representative sample, increase the probability that a study will be informative.[2] Rosenthal (1990) expressed an optimistic note regarding the changes that are taking place in how statistics are used to test a hypothesis:

> The good news is that more sophisticated editors, referees, and researchers are becoming aware that reporting the results of a significance test is not a sufficiently enlightening procedure to stand alone. More and more we are beginning to see a report of the magnitude of the effect accompanying the *p* level. (p. 775)

---

[2]Two other methods of data analysis that deserve mention are Cohen's (1988) U (a measure of nonoverlap in scores between two samples) and McGraw and Wong's (1992) common language effect size indicator (CL). CL is a measure of probability "that a score sampled at random from one distribution will be greater than a score sampled from some other distribution" (p. 361).

Motivation and Knowledge of the Publication Process

Another critical feature that Nobel Laureates exhibit is a persistence and determination in their research efforts once an important problem has come into focus. These individuals "exhibit a great capacity to tolerate frustration in their work, absorbing repeated failures without manifest psychological damage" (Merton, 1963/1973, p. 453). The first frustration an author must be prepared for is the high probability that his or her manuscript will be rejected for publication by the first one or two journals to which it is submitted. Additionally, even if the paper is accepted, it will require revisions prior to publication.

Chief Editorial Advisor for APA's Publications and Communications Board Dorothy Eichorn and Executive Director for Publications and Communications at APA Gary VandenBos (1985) have classified publication decision making for APA journals in three areas. The first class consists of manuscript acceptance without revision. This occurs for approximately 2% of papers submitted to APA journals. The remaining 98% of manuscripts are rejected. According to Eichorn and Vandenbos (1985), authors who receive a letter from the editor informing them that their paper is rejected, but are offered the opportunity to revise and resubmit, are actually receiving a positive response. Most manuscripts ultimately accepted for publication by APA journals are those initially rejected, with the comment that the author may "revise and resubmit."

The third category of editorial response is outright rejection. Rick Crandall (1987), editor of the *Journal of Social and Behavioral Psychology*, suggested that arguing with an editor about the decision to reject a paper does not help an author's cause. John Campbell (1982/1985), editor of the *Journal of Applied Psychology*, noted that of 3,636 papers submitted in his 6 years as editor, *none* were accepted without revisions, and David Weiss (1989), editor of *Applied Psychological Measurement*, reported that four or five revisions of a paper is common.

If a paper is revised and resubmitted, it is advantageous to state in a cover letter to the editor, point by point, pages where changes were made and how each reviewer's criticism has been addressed. If an author decides not to alter the content in spite of peer reviewer criticism, it is best to inform the editor of this and state the rationale. Both editors and reviewers are impressed by efforts to accommodate reviewers' suggested alterations (Berardo, 1980; Eichorn & VandenBos, 1985; Greenwald, 1987).

Another simple procedure for increasing the probability of having a quality paper accepted for publication is to avoid exceeding the page length limitations stated by the journal (Eichorn & VandenBos, 1985). Typically, for APA journals, three to four typed pages equals one published page (Cameron, 1990). Former editors of the *Journal of Experimental Social Psychology* recommended that "it is definitely a disadvantage to add length just to give a reviewer a chance to argue for shortening it. Long papers put reviewers in bad moods" (Wyer, Greenwald, Bernard, Crandall, & Anonymous, 1987, p. 13).

Anthony Greenwald (1987), former editor of the *Journal of Personality and Social Psychology*, advised that an author "make sure that the first paper you submit to a given editor is a strong one. That is the tactic that is most likely to lead the editor subsequently to be biased in your favor" (p. 15).

Another potentially frustrating aspect of the publication process is the length of time it takes for an author to perform a research study and finally see it in print. Garvey, Lin, and Tomita (1979) questioned over 3,000 scientists and engineers on this issue. They reported that it takes about 13 months to perform the research, write the paper, and submit it. Once submitted, it takes an additional 15 months to have it appear in print. Thus, it may take approximately 2½ years from commencing research to reaching print. If being published is part of the incentive for conducting research, the experimenter must anticipate long intervals of "delay of gratification." To reduce discouragement, it is essential that authors be aware of the obstacles that are likely to occur in the journal publication process.

For behavioral scientists, Cowen, Spinell, Hightower, and Lotyczewski (1987) found that for seven psychology journals, 5 months was the average lag time between initial submission of a paper to submission of the revised manuscript. Approximately 90% of APA journals take 4 months from time of submission to notification that the manuscript is accepted (usually contingent upon revision) or rejected. However, this time lag is greater for papers submitted between spring through summer (April 15—August 15) and during Christmas through New Years (November 5—December 31) (Eichorn & VandenBos, 1985).

The core of publication decision making resides in the peer review system, which has been the most intensely debated aspect of the journal publication process. The editor of the *Journal of the American Medical Association* (JAMA), Drummond Rennie (1990), stated that publication is the heart of scientific process and peer review is the heart of the publication process. In May, 1989, JAMA sponsored The First International Congress on Peer Review in Biomedical Publications. "Scientific investigations in this field were woefully lacking, and we set out to change this state of affairs" (Rennie, 1990, p. 1317). Over 300 people from 22 countries participated in the conference. Approximately two thirds of the participants were journal editors.

Peer review involves the practice of having professionals in a field judge the quality of a manuscript submission (Cicchetti, 1991; Zuckerman & Merton, 1971). Usually the peer reviewer (also termed referee) will make recommendations to the editor that a paper either be published (usually with revisions that the reviewer has stated in the critique) or not be published. Peer reviewers provide up to six major functions:

1. They provide expert judgment regarding the scientific quality of a manuscript.

2. They protect the editor from many negative reactions authors of rejected papers might exhibit.

3. They provide suggestions for how the manuscript might be improved.

4. They can sometimes offer authors information on how their work is related to other studies in the field.

5. Through their knowledge of a discipline, reviewers can inform editors if the submission is too similar to other papers already published.

6. Acceptance of a paper in a peer review journal is an informal means by which the work is judged as meeting scientifically acceptable standards. (Zuckerman & Merton, 1971)

There is a symbiotic relationship between the influence editors have over reviewers and that of reviewers on editors. The decision whether to forward a submission to a peer reviewer rests entirely with the journal editor (Roediger, 1987). An editor may accept or—more likely—reject a paper outright. The editor decides which peer reviewers to select and the number of referees needed. The editor of the *American Anthropologist* remarked: "It is really quite simple for me as an editor to guarantee that an article will be killed by referees. All I need to do is to select referees I know can be trusted to clobber a particular manuscript" (Bernard, 1982, p. 202). After reviewers have been selected and the paper critiqued, it is the editor's decision whether to accept the suggestions for revisions made by the reviewer as well as the recommendations to accept or reject the paper for publication.

Studies involving the influences peer reviewers have over editors' decision making, although few in number, suggest editors frequently institute reviewers' advice. For the *American Sociological Review*, there was a correlation of .81 between the reviewers' recommendation to accept or reject a manuscript and that of the editor's ultimate decision (Bakanic, McPhail, & Simon, 1987, cited in Cicchetti, 1991). Editors of medical journals ($N = 102$) reported that when two or more reviewers agree to accept or reject a submission, they will follow the recommendation 85% of the time (Weller, 1990). For the journal *Thorax*, there was a 100% rate of publication acceptance if both reviewers recommended that a paper be published. Similarly, if both reviewers rejected the submission, the paper was never published. For split reviewer decisions, the manuscript was published 10% of the time (Lock, 1985, cited in Cicchetti, 1991).

For 996 manuscripts submitted to the *Journal of Abnormal Psychology*, there was a 72% chance of acceptance when either both reviewers recommended publication or when one reviewer recommended acceptance upon revision and the other referee judged the paper acceptable without revision. If both reviewers suggested the paper be revised and resubmitted, there was a 27% chance of the manuscript being published. All other combinations of peer reviewer judgments resulted in an acceptance rate of less than 6% (Cicchetti, 1991).

Lindsey (1977) studied "editorial power," which he defined as the percentage of manuscripts a reviewer recommends for publication that the editor does, in fact, decide to publish. Lindsey reported that the number of articles a reviewer has published positively relates to editorial power (beta weight = .406), but the number of citations a reviewer's articles receive is negatively associated with editorial influence (beta weight = −.456).

Because careers, status, and promotions rest on journal publications, and having a paper accepted for publication depends largely on the judgment of peer reviewers, there has been widespread concern over the fairness of the system. Approximately 33% of published researchers believe that authors' publication records and/or the status of their institutional affiliation affect publication decision making irrespective of a paper's content (Kupfersmid & Fiala, 1991). Studies of reviewers' attitudes on this issue lend support to the contention that this form of bias exists.

Forty-one percent of a sample of reviewers for Canadian journals in the behavioral sciences ($N = 193$) stated they are more likely to recommend a manuscript for publication if they believe the author has a good reputation (Rowney & Zenisek, 1980). Thirty percent of the editors from 19 management journals ($N = 283$) claimed that a recommendation for publication acceptances increases if they attribute a positive reputation to the author (Kerr et al., 1977). Additionally, 40% of the editors of medical journals ($N = 102$) stated that an author's prestige and institutional affiliation are likely to affect their judgment of publication worthiness (Weller, 1990).

Perlman (1982) argued that bias based on prestige of the author and/or institutional affiliation is appropriate because high-status authors write better articles. He presented evidence from two studies. In the first study, he selected 60 articles from the *Journal of Abnormal Psychology* (which does not employ blind review). Based on Roose and Anderson's ratings of university status, half the articles selected were from authors at highly prestigious institutions, and half from nonprestigious institutions.

Perlman used citation frequency as the measure of article quality. The mean citation rate for articles written by "high-status" authors was 3.79; for "low-status" authors the mean citation rate per article was 1.40. He repeated this study with 60 articles, written by authors of high and low status institutions, that were published in the *Journal of Personality and Social Psychology* (which uses blind review). The "high-status" authors' articles had a mean citation rate of 9.52; "low-status" authors had a mean citation rate of 2.56 per article.

Perlman's (1982) data support his position to the extent that Roose and Anderson's rating of universities (measured by reputational judgments made by department of psychology chairpersons) is accepted as a valid measure of institutional status and frequency of citation is accepted as a convincing measure of quality. There has, however, been considerable debate regarding the use of reputational ratings and employing citations as a measure of article quality. (See Chapter Five for a discussion of this problem.)

Results discrepant with Perlman's findings were reported by Mahoney, Kazdin, and Kenigsberg (1978). These authors examined rate of acceptance for publication of manuscripts as a function of self-citations and institutional prestige (nature of measure not stated). Reviewers ($N = 68$) from two behavioristically oriented journals served as subjects. The authors reported that self-citation increased the probability of manuscript acceptance but author's institutional affiliation had no such relationship. Similarly, Schaeffer (1970) examined the issue of whether editors of behavioral science journals are biased towards accepting manuscripts submitted by "friends" for publication. Friends were defined as individuals who work in the same institution as the editor. The results suggest that editors are not biased towards accepting a disproportionate number of papers submitted by friends for publication.

Current data indicate that about 33% of researchers believe publication bias exists as a function of an author's individual status and/or affiliated institutional prestige. A similar proportion of reviewers endorsed the notion of being biased. In an effort to reduce the taint of bias, the practice of blind review has become popular. This involves having the editor remove the title page of a manuscript which directly identifies the author's name and affiliation. Available data indicate that there is support for the continued use of blind reviews, but the support is not overwhelming. In a survey of members of Division 14 of APA (Industrial/Organizational), 63% ($N = 203$) endorsed the use of blind review (Mitchell, Beach, & Smith, 1985). Fifty-six percent of peer reviewers ($N = 193$) also favor its continued use (Rowney & Zenisek, 1980). Others have argued against the use of blind review, stating that it does not increase fairness, it deprives reviewers of important information, and reviewers can often detect the author's identity in spite of it (Ceci & Peters, 1984).

Approximately 70% ($N = 132$) of psychologists believe a peer reviewer can correctly detect the author of a paper regardless of blind review (Ceci & Peters, 1984). Seventy-six percent of the members of the Psychonomic Society ($N = 265$) believe reviewers can correctly determine authorship under blind review procedures (Bradley, 1981). When questioned, peer reviewers ($N = 153$) stated they made accurate author detections 37% of the time (Rowney & Zenisek, 1980).

Three studies have directly investigated reviewers' accuracy in detecting authorship under blind review conditions. For peer reviewers of behavioral science journals ($N = 146$), 26% correctly identified the author(s) of submitted papers (Ceci & Peters, 1984); for peer reviews of medical journals, 58% correctly identified the author(s) (McNutt, Evans, Flecher, & Flecher, 1990); and, for the most prestigious journal in physics, *Physical Review Letters*, peer reviewers correctly identified 80% of the authors (Adair, 1982). Thus, the accuracy with which a peer reviewer can identify an author correctly when the reviewer is "blind" is variable across different domains of science.

The critical concern, however, is whether knowledge of an author's identity and/or institutional affiliation results in differential acceptance-rejection rates for papers submitted for publication. We have been able to find only two studies that have addressed this issue. Crane (1967) studied differences in institutional status among authors of three sociology journals, one of which practiced blind review. She noted that there was no relationship between blind/unblind review and institutional status among journal authors. The best study located on this issue was that of McNutt et al. (1990). These authors randomly selected manuscripts from the *Journal of General Internal Medicine* in which one half of the referees were under blind review and the other one half reviewed the same manuscripts unblindly. Blinding prevented author detection in 73% of the manuscripts reviewed. Reviewers who were blinded were rated by editors as providing better quality reviews ($M = 3.5$) than those unblinded ($M = 3.1$). Most important, "blinded and unblinded reviewers did not differ in their recommendations regarding whether to accept the manuscript for publication" (p. 1374).

It is not clear whether author/institutional status differentially influences publication acceptance/rejection. The paucity of data suggests that there is great variability between the fields of science in the degree of accurate detection of authorship. However, even if authorship is identifiable, there is little evidence linking such information to acceptance/ rejection bias among peer reviewers. This conclusion is offered in spite of the sizable percentage of peer reviewers who contend that being influenced by author/institutional status is a legitimate form of bias.

Recently, evidence has been accumulating suggesting that an insidious form of peer reviewer bias exists. This bias is impervious to blind review and has been labeled *confirmatory* bias, which is defined as the tendency to support, remember, and/or confirm ideas already held to be true (Mahoney, 1977). Goodstein and Brazis (1970) assumed that the majority of psychologists do not attribute validity to astrological predictions. They sent an abstract of a study investigating astrological predictions to randomly selected psychologists ($N = 282$). Approximately one half of the sample received an abstract that demonstrated the accuracy of astrological prediction and one half of the sample received an abstract where the prediction was not supported. Psychologists who received the negative outcome abstract rated this study as better designed, having greater validity, and providing a more relevant conclusion than those who received the statistically significant finding. (There is, of course, some rationale to the notion that studies supporting astrological accuracy are, in fact, less valid.) This study also suggests that confirmatory bias may be more potent than the bias against publishing negative results.

Smith et al. (1980) investigated the ES reported by scientists judged as being positive towards psychotherapy's effectiveness versus those rated antagonistic towards the benefit of psychotherapy. Studies published by proponents of psychotherapy reported an average ES of 0.95 (SD = 1.45); for those antagonistic to psychotherapy, the average ES reported in psychotherapy outcome studies was 0.66 (SD = 0.77). When an author's bias was judged as "balanced" or "unknown," the average reported ES was 0.78 (SD = 0.86).

The most convincing data on the existence of confirmatory bias come from Mahoney's (1977) study. In that experiment all reviewers (N = 67) were sent a manuscript with the same Introduction and Methods sections. Some reviewers received this manuscript with a Results section that provided data supporting their theoretical orientation (positive results), others received a Results section where the data did not support their theoretical orientation (negative results), and some reviewers received a Results section containing a mixed outcome. A fourth group of reviewers did not receive a Results section at all.

As part of standard procedure for the *Journal of Applied Behavior Analysis*, all reviewers rated each manuscript's quality on a one through six scale. Each reviewer provided the editor with one of four recommendations: accept for publication, accept with minor revisions, accept with major revisions, and reject. Referees were blind to the identity of the author and to the author's institutional affiliation. The results were:

1. There was no difference across reviewers in their judgment of "Topic Relevance."

2. Those receiving a Results section confirming their theoretical persuasion rated the methodology section and the "Data Presentation" section higher than reviewers who received a Results section discrepant from their theoretical orientation.

3. Rating of the manuscript's "Scientific Contribution" also was affected by confirmatory bias. The mean rating for manuscripts with results supporting a reviewer's theoretical orientation was appreciably higher (M = 4.3) from that of those in which the Results section disconfirmed the reviewers' respective theoretical positions (M = 2.4). For those referees who did not have a Results section available, ratings of the "Scientific Contribution" of the manuscript were similar to reviewers receiving data supporting their theoretical bias (M = 4.5).

The critical dependent variable, of course, was that which is most relevant to publication—namely, the reviewer's Summary Recommendation. . . . Identical manuscripts suffered very different fates depending on the direction of their data. When they were positive, the usual recommendation was to accept with moderate revisions. Negative results earned a significantly lower evaluation, with the average reviewer urging either rejection or major revision. Referees who were not given any results were much more generous in their recommendations than reviewers who read a results section. Mixed results manuscripts were consistently rejected without any apparent influence by their manner of interpretation. (Mahoney, 1977, p. 170)

Those affirming the existence of confirmatory bias in the peer review process, thus far, have presented evidence supporting its actuality. Again, however, there are few studies in the area. Part of the problem is that "editors can turn down research on reviewing, claiming that there is not sufficient data to show biased or unreliable reviewing, yet they themselves have actively blocked the collection of such data" (Spencer, Hartnett, & Mahoney, 1986, p. 33). When confirmatory bias is added to the "bias equation" (which includes the bias for the use of statistical significance, the bias against negative outcomes, and the bias against publishing replication studies), the data presented in the behavioral science literature take another step down on the scale of credibility and empirical objectivity.

One of the most disconcerting experiences an author faces is having a manuscript rejected for publication, in spite of the fact that one of the critiques of the paper is positive. As previously noted, when *both* reviewers recommend publication, there is a 75% to 85% chance the editor will agree with the reviewers' recommendation. However, a paper is rarely published when reviews are mixed. In this section the research on interrater agreement among referees will be summarized to obtain an estimate of how often authors can expect to receive different opinions among reviewers regarding the quality of their work.

One of the highly debated topics in the literature concerns which statistics are most appropriate to employ as a measure of interrater agreement. Reviewer agreement/reliability is defined "as the extent to which two or more independent reviewers of the same scientific document agree" (Cicchetti, 1991, p. 120). In spite of Whitehurst's (1984) advocacy of the use of Finn's r, the consensus is to employ kappa (K) with a dichotomous rating, such as accept versus reject. If three or more reviewers are used, the intraclass correlation coefficient (R_I) is recommended (Cicchetti, 1980, 1991; Rosenthal, 1991c). Kappa and R_I are equivalent to a Pearson product-moment correlation (Rosenthal, 1991c).

The majority of studies on interrater agreement analyze reviewer correspondence by either K or R_I. The most thorough review of literature on the subject has been conducted by Cicchetti (1991), who reported interrater agreement exclusively in K or R_I terms.

Table 2 summarizes the extent of agreement among peer reviewers in psychology, sociology, and biomedical journals. Generally, the correlation between peer reviewers across psychology, sociology, and biomedical journals ranges from about .25 to .35 (Cicchetti, 1991).[3] The degree of agreement is slightly greater when authors have been allowed to nominate peer reviewers for their papers. Gottfredson (1978) requested authors ($N = 687$) who had published articles in nine psychology journals to select three professionals they felt qualified to judge their articles. Authors' nominees ($N = 540$) rated papers on a 36-item scale. Paired agreement of experts' opinions regarding the article's quality was $R_I = .41$; the agreement among reviewers' judgment of article impact was $R_I = .35$.

In addition to referees' global ratings of a manuscript, Cicchetti (1991) surveyed the literature on agreement between reviewers by evaluation of subcategory of manuscript characteristics. This (sparse) literature is summarized in Table 3.

Examination of these data suggests the average $R_I = .26$, with a range of .19 to .32. Thus, reviewers have a higher probability of agreeing on the global quality (acceptance/rejection) of a manuscript than on any specific manuscript characteristic measured thus far. There has been considerable debate regarding the interpretation of these data. Some argue that the numbers indicate satisfactory interrater agreement. Others believe that they reflect randomness and error variance in the peer review process (Cicchetti, 1991; Crandall, 1978; Marsh & Ball, 1981).

Agreement among referees for grant proposals has also been studied. Again, Cicchetti (1991) has provided a comprehensive summary. Data from Table 4 suggest that these correlations are very similar to

---

[3]Rosenthal (1991a) recommended that the Spearman-Brown formula be employed to determine the reliability between judges' ratings. Rosenthal terms this the "effective reliability" and provides a table that transforms reliability estimates into effective reliabilities. Thus, when three judges are involved and the obtained reliability coefficient is .30, the effective reliability becomes .56.

Table 2
Summary of Peer Reviewer Agreement in Psychology, Sociology, and Biomedical Journals

Name of journal	Correlation
Psychology journals	
Social Problems	.40[a]
Journal of Personality & Social Psychology	.26[b]
Sociometry	.21[b]
Personality & Social Psychology Bulletin	.21[b]
Journal of Abnormal Psychology	.19[b]
American Psychologist	.54[b]
American Psychologist	.38[b]
Journal of Educational Psychology	.34[b]
Developmental Review	.44[b]
Median correlation	.34
Sociology journals	
American Sociological Review	.29[b]
Law & Society Review	.23[b]
Median correlation	.26
Biomedical journals	
New England Journal of Medicine	.26[a]
British Journal of Medicine	.31[a]
Physiological Zoology	.31[b]
Median correlation	.31

Summary data is based on Cicchetti (1991).
[a]Kappan correlation coefficient.
[b]Intraclass correlation coefficient.

the relationship measuring reviewer agreement in articles published in journals in psychology, sociology, and biomedicine. Another way to look at these data is to examine the percentage of time that one reviewer decides to accept an article for publication and the second reviewer agrees. Data are available for three psychology journals. For the *Journal of Abnormal Psychology*, when one reviewer recommends that a paper be accepted for publication, the second reviewer agrees 47% of the

Table 3
Peer Review Agreement (R₁) of Journal Articles by Subcategory

Subcategory	Journal				
	JAP[a]	*JPSP*[b]	*BJM*[c]	*AASLD*[d]	*Mdn*
Importance	.23	.28	.33	.24	.26
Design	.32	.19[e]	—	.29	.29
Data analysis	.22	—	—	—	.22
Style & organization	.22	.25	—	—	.24
Literature review	.26	.37	—	—	.32
Reader interest	.19	.07	.22[f]	—	.19
Succinctness	.30	.31	—	—	.31
Originality	—	—	.21	.30	.26
Total					.26

Data based on Cicchetti (1991).
[a] *Journal of Abnormal Psychology.*
[b] *Journal of Personality and Social Psychology.*
[c] *British Journal of Medicine.*
[d] *American Association for the Study of Liver Disease.*
[e] Actual subcategory used was "Design and Analysis."
[f] Actual subcategory used was "Suitability."

Table 4
Summary of Peer Reviewer Agreement (R₁) for Grant Proposals

	Discipline		
	Chemical dynamics	*Solid state physics*	*Economics*
NSF[a] open review	.25	.32	.37
COSPUP[b] open review	.32	.34	.36
COSPUP blind review	.18	.33	.37

Data reported by Cicchetti (1991).
[a] National Science Foundation.
[b] Committee on Science and Public Policy of the National Academy of Sciences.

time; there is a 50% rate of agreement for two referees assessing manuscripts submitted to *Developmental Review*; and for the *American Psychologist* there is a 66% chance that both reviewers will recommend acceptance (Cicchetti, 1991).

Similar studies have been conducted on agreement between reviewers to accept grant proposals from both NSF and COSPUP. In the field of chemical dynamics, there is a 54% chance that both referees will agree to fund a grant application; in economics and solid state physics there is a 60% rate of agreement in this area. The magnitude of referee agreement across such "soft" sciences as psychology and economics is consistent with the degree of peer reviewer agreement in the "hard" sciences such as biology, medicine, chemical dynamics, and solid state physics (Cicchetti, 1991).

Data are also available when percentage of agreement is examined from the perspective of both reviewers rejecting a manuscript and/or grant proposal. When one reviewer rejects a manuscript for publication from the *Journal of Abnormal Psychology*, there is a 70% chance the second reviewer will also reject the paper; for *Developmental Review* there is a 76% agreement on rejected papers; and, for the *American Psychologist* the level of agreement is 78%. For grant proposals in chemical dynamics there is a 70% agreement on proposal rejection among reviewers; for economics the rejection agreement is 83%; and for solid state physics agreement to reject a proposal among reviewers is 73% (Cicchetti, 1991). Reaching a consensus regarding the scientific quality of a research study seems to be comparable across many disciplines of science regardless of the extent to which a "grand paradigm" exists.

John Campbell (1982/1985), former editor of *Applied Psychology*, claimed that agreement among reviewers could be higher, but editors often select referees with different areas of expertise. Thus, "there is no way a correlation between raters can be regarded as a reliability coefficient" (p. 326). However, it is unclear why, for example, an expert in statistical analysis versus an expert in the content of a study would have greatly discrepant views on whether a study is relevant and well designed. It is our contention that a great deal of the unaccounted-for variance in reviewer agreement is due to the effect that the research outcome has on judges' opinions.

Authors seem to have a love–hate relationship with peer reviewers. A researcher's only communication with a peer reviewer is by reading the reviewer's critique of his or her paper. As previously noted, a typical manuscript represents about a year's work for a scientist (Garvey et al., 1979), yet some reviewers' assessments of the manuscript are not only negative, but written in an insensitive tone (Bradley, 1981).

Referees' feedback to authors is not in the form of a reliability statistic but rather a qualitative report of which the contents, structure, and length are greatly determined by the reviewer. Fiske and Fogg (1990) studied free response comments made by peer reviewers for papers submitted to 12 editors of APA journals. Comments by referees were coded with judges agreeing 79% of the time on what code best applied. The researchers compared points of criticism for peer reviewer pairs on 585 manuscripts.

There were only 31 matches of points of criticism between reviewers beyond what would be expected by chance (R_1 = .20). In effect, the feedback given to authors by reviewers often appears highly inconsistent. An author may have the feeling that peer reviewers are not even reading the same paper. Nisbett (1978)—perhaps tongue-in-cheek—claimed that "any reviewer worth his or her salt can think up as good a theoretical position as the author's in a few minutes' time" (p. 520).

The average time it takes an author to revise a paper is 20 hours (Cowen et al., 1987). The high percentage of manuscripts that require revision prior to publication acceptance has been a sore point for some researchers. As stated earlier, of 3,636 papers submitted to the *Journal of Applied Psychology, none* was accepted without revision (Campbell, 1982/1985). Bradley (1982) reported that 15 *former editors* of the *Journal of the American Statistical Association* (JASA) submitted papers to this journal of which *all* required revision. "It is hard to believe that virtually none of the contributors to JASA can write a publishable article without help and even harder to believe that serving several years as editor of the journal does nothing to remedy this situation" (p. 272).

One of the most controversial studies conducted on the peer review process was that of Peters and Ceci (1982). They submitted 12 "papers" for publication which were actually articles previously published by the journal to which the papers were submitted. Three of the submissions were detected, eight of the remaining nine manuscripts were rejected. This finding alone raises many questions about chance operating in the peer review system of publication decision making. Crandall (1987) concluded that "the lack of reliability and validity in the editorial review system is a professional disgrace" (p. 408). Knoll (1990) contended that "one of the greatest frustrations of attempting to study peer review is the total lack of outcome measures. Does interreviewer agreement tell us anything more than that the reviewers share the same sets of prejudices?" (p. 1330). Bornstein (1991a) added:

The American Psychological Association's *Standards for Educational and Psychological Testing* reveals that peer review fails miserably with respect to *every* technical criterion for establishing the reliability and validity of an assessment instrument. If one attempted to publish research involving an assessment tool whose reliability and validity data were as weak as that of the peer review process, there is no question that studies involving this psychometrically flawed instrument would be deemed unacceptable for publication. (p. 139)

The editor of the *Journal of Personality and Individual Difference*, H. J. Eysenck (1980), has become so disenchanted with the peer review process that he has eliminated it entirely.

Given the high frequency of inconsistent feedback authors experience when reading peer reviewers' evaluations, it is not surprising that approximately 75% of researchers endorse the statement: "Acceptance or rejection for publication is often due to which reviewer(s) happens to be selected to evaluate the manuscript" (Kupfersmid & Fiala, 1991, p. 249). Kupfersmid and Fiala (1990) labeled this the "crap shoot hypothesis." Analysis of peer reviewer agreement for grant proposals led Cole, Cole, and Simon (1981) to a similar judgment:

We conclude that the funding of a specific proposal submitted to the NSF is to a significant extent dependent on the applicant's luck in the program director's choice of reviewers. . . . Clearly the more proposals a researcher submits the higher the probability of being funded. In fact, eminent scientists may be more likely to be funded than less well-known ones not because their probability of success is greater for each submitted proposal, but because they submit many proposals and are not deterred by an individual rejection. (p. 885)

Support for the "crap shoot hypothesis" is also apparent when acceptance/rejection rates are analyzed. Approximately 25% of articles submitted to APA journals are accepted for publication (Eichorn & VandenBos, 1985). As previously noted, based on approximately 1,000 manuscripts submitted to the *Journal of Abnormal Psychology*, if two reviewers both recommend that a paper be published, there is a 72% chance that the editor will agree. If both reviewers recommend rejection, an editor will almost always not publish the paper. Finally, there is approximately a 6% chance that a paper will be published if the reviews are mixed (Cicchetti, 1991). The APA Committee on Women in Psychology (1980) reported that 73% of the time for both APA and non-APA journals, two reviewers are selected to evaluate a manuscript.

The "crap shoot hypothesis" maintains that which papers are published is a chance event contingent on which reviewers are selected. If there is a 50–50 chance of any given reviewer recommending a manuscript's acceptance for publication, the following scenario is likely:

1. For any 100 manuscripts, by chance alone, two reviewers will agree that 25 of these papers should be published (.5 × .5 = .25).

2. Of these 25 papers, the editor will actually publish 17 of them (25 × .72 = 17).

3. By chance alone there will be mixed reviews for 50 papers submitted of which three will be accepted for print by the editor (50 × .06 = 3).

4. Thus, if peer reviewer evaluation of acceptance or rejection is a coin flip, for every 100 manuscripts submitted approximately 20 would be accepted for publication. Actually, this percentage would be slightly higher because 27% of the submissions were accepted for publication when both reviewers for the *Journal of Abnormal Psychology* recommended "revise and resubmit" (Cicchetti, 1991). However, it is unclear what percentage of manuscripts submitted fall in this category.

The percentage of manuscripts accepted for publication on the basis of a peer review "crap shoot" (probably a more accurate term would be "coin flip hypothesis") is uncomfortably close to what is observed in APA journal publications. The peer review process is not without ardent defenders, however. Some have noted that being an editor or peer reviewer is a thankless job. Eichorn and VandenBos (1985) reported that between 50% to 80% of those asked to edit APA journals decline the invitation. The offer is rejected in spite of APA journals being judged as very high in prestige regardless of what method of rating is employed (see Chapter Five).

Peer reviewers work without financial compensation, and the time it takes to critique a paper can be considerable. Peer reviewer evaluations for the *Journal of Public Health* report that 150 minutes is the average time it takes to critique a manuscript (Yankauer, 1990). Referees for the *British Medical Journal* report an average evaluation time of 80 minutes. For papers written in the field of pediatrics, the average time is 70 minutes, while for papers addressing psychiatric issues the average reviewer time is 86 minutes (Lock & Smith, 1990). Finke (1990) reported that it is very difficult to harness experts in the field to perform peer review.

Data from several studies have consistently demonstrated that a sizable majority of professionals in the behavioral sciences are supportive of the peer review system. For Kupfersmid and Fiala's (1991) sample of published authors ($N = 68$), 61% endorsed the statement that the "present method of determining which manuscripts are selected to be published is generally satisfactory" (p. 249). When members of APA ($N = 158$), the Psychonomic Society ($N = 140$), and members of the American Statistical Association ($N = 113$) were questioned, 75% believed scientific progress would decrease in the absence of peer review. In a separate survey of Psychonomic Society members only, 87% reported that peer reviewers' suggestions enhance the quality of a paper; 60% felt that referees are open-minded; and, 78% believed referees are competent (Bradley, 1981).

One of the most telling findings is from surveys of authors who have had their papers rejected by peer reviewers. For Garvey et al.'s (1979) sample of over 3,000 scientists and engineers, approximately 50% of those who are informed their paper is rejected revise it before submitting the paper to another journal. For behavioral scientists, 75% report that if their manuscript is rejected they will revise it before resubmission (Kupfersmid & Fiala, 1991). Seventy-two percent of APA members, as well as members of the Psychonomic Society and the American Statistical Association, who have had their last submission rejected, reported that the peer reviewers' suggestions were helpful (Bradley, 1981). A majority of surveyed authors who had to revise and resubmit papers ($N = 483$) rated reviewers' suggestions as "moderately important and insightful" (Cowen et al., 1987, p. 404). And, finally, 83% of Kupfersmid and Fiala's (1991) sample of behavioral scientists reported that at least 50% of reviewers' criticisms are helpful.

Fletcher (1991) considered peer reviewer reliability or satisfaction/dissatisfaction a moot issue because the majority of studies are eventually published anyway. A review of the relevant data supports his position. Psychonomic Society members report that 77% of their published articles were rejected at least by one journal (Bradley, 1981). Similarly, 77% of the members of the Academy of Management and members of the Society of Organizational Behavior ($N = 203$) reported that papers submitted to academy management journals are ultimately published (Mitchell et al., 1985). In a survey of psychology faculty members ($N = 368$), it was reported that 87% of their manuscripts are accepted for publication (Lipsey, 1974). In the behavioral sciences in general, 75% to 85% of manuscripts submitted are published if the authors are persistent.

Figures comparable to these are evident for authors submitting to biomedical journals. Wilson (1978, cited in Cicchetti, 1991) reported that 85% of the papers rejected by *The New England Journal of Medicine* or the *Journal of Clinical Investigation* are ultimately published in other journals. Lock (1985; cited in Cicchetti, 1991) found that 68% of the rejected papers from the *British Medical Journal* are eventually published.

Researchers' ambivalence about the peer review system and their endorsement of the "crap shoot hypothesis" in such high numbers seems to be a result of their direct experience with publication decision making. For any given manuscript, the majority of authors can expect peer reviewer feedback which is either very positive (all reviewers like the manuscript) or quasi-positive (at least one reviewer likes the paper) at some point in the submission process. This may be the impetus for an author to continue submitting the paper (usually in revised form as a function of referee comment) to other journals. If a paper continues to be submitted, the odds are very likely it will be accepted by some journal. Because the majority of papers will be accepted for publication, an author may logically conclude it is not the quality of the manuscript that determines acceptance, but the luck of the draw in the editor-peer reviewer selection process. Thus, authors may become disgruntled because peer reviewers are deemed responsible for rejecting their "masterpiece," yet be satisfied because it is often recognized as publishable by the peer review system.

We agree with Roediger's (1987) reasoning for continued use of the peer review system, in spite of its flaws. Roediger contends: "We must paraphrase the statement often applied to democracy: 'Peer review is the worst form of scientific evaluation, except for all others that have been tried' " (p. 239). Additionally, we support Armstrong's (1982) position that the practice of blind review should continue because there have been no data which demonstrate that it is harmful, and the cost of the process is negligible.

5 GETTING PUBLISHED IN BETTER JOURNALS

Approximately 300 professional journals publish articles that focus on psychological content (American Psychological Association, 1988); approximately 200 journals publish articles related to the field of sociology (McCartney, 1976); and, Broad and Wade (1982b) estimated the existence of 8,000 biomedical journals. Data presented in Chapter Four indicate that the great majority of papers submitted for publication ultimately appear in print. In the behavioral sciences, 75% to 85% of manuscripts submitted for publication are published; in the biomedical field this figure ranges from 68% to 85%.

It was pointed out in Chapter One that getting a manuscript accepted for publication is not difficult. However, being published in a "better" journal (one that is rated highly on at least one of three impact factors) is not so easy. These impact factors are:

1. the impact of citation—articles in these journals are more likely to be cited as references in other journal articles.
2. the impact of subjective prestige—professionals in the field rank these journals as publishing the best articles.
3. the impact of readership—these journals have the highest circulation rates among professional publications.

Being published in a better journal brings attention to an article. Authors want to have their names associated with quality and with helping to find answers to important problems. Likewise, universities want their name identified with the most consequential findings in the field. As a result, there have been several attempts to rate the quality of graduate programs in psychology on the basis of their faculty's publications (Cox & Catt, 1977; Endler, Rushton, & Roediger, 1978; Howard, Cole, & Maxwell, 1989). In the endless search for individual (as well as institutional) recognition, it is to a researcher's benefit to publish in a journal that maintains a positive image. And when deciding to which journal one will submit a manuscript, it is recommended that an author select a journal that is rated high on at least one of these three impact factors.

Citation Impact and Journal Rankings

Lindsey (1978) presented a rationale for the use of citation counts as a measure of journal quality. "If the work occurring in a given field is leading to a cumulative body of knowledge, then reference trails among the work of the contributors will be left in the form of citations" (p. 129). Some researchers believe that citation counts are more objective and relatively free of bias. Myers (1970) constructed a cumulative frequency distribution of author citations for articles published in psychology journals from 1962 through 1967. He provided evidence that citation counts are a valid measure of author competency by noting the following:

1. Thus far, only three psychologists have won the National Medal of Science and all three are at the 99th percentile for citation counts.
2. Of eight psychologists listed in *Modern Men of Science*, seven are above the 90th percentile in citation counts.
3. The 98th percentile in citation counts represents the median for the past 20 presidents of APA.
4. Of the 42 psychologists receiving the Distinguished Scientific Contribution Award, the 97th percentile is this group's median citation ranking.
5. The 95th percentile is the median citation ranking for 50 psychologists selected between 1950 and 1967 as members of the Society of Experimental Psychology, an elite group of researchers.

6. For psychology department chairpersons' selection of the 10 most influential living psychologists, all have citation rates at or above the 89th percentile.

Garfield (1972) studied citation frequencies of journal articles across a wide range of scientific fields. He found that a core of 152 journals accounted for 50% of the references to all areas of the sciences studied. For all scientific papers the average number of citations is 1.7 (Garfield, 1972). In the behavioral sciences, the average paper is cited about once (Matson et al., 1989). Garfield also studied a journal's impact factor (i.e., the frequency with which articles in a given journal are referenced), after correction for the number of articles the journal publishes, per year. The two psychology journals with the highest impact factor are *Psychological Review* and *Psychological Bulletin*.

The use of citation counts as a measure of quality of research has its detractors. Lindsey (1978) noted that (a) little is known about how scientists select what to cite, (b) often an important paper is unrecognized until long after it is published, (c) studies have shown that elementary statistical textbooks are cited with great frequency, and (d) citation counts are sensitive to fads (e.g., *Future Shock* was one of the most highly referenced publications in the 1970s), and (e) scientists seem to use citation counts as a measure of quality because citation is easily measurable. Lindsey concluded:

> In reading the literature in the sociology of science, one finds that authors talking about citations shift to citation counts as measures of quality, and then to the discussion of quality, on the assumption that quality is determined by a count of citations. (p. 137)

Thorne (1977) added that researchers cite more prestigious authors more frequently because they believe this is more likely to impress reviewers. Some support for this position is evident in Evans, Nadjari, and Burchell's (1990) investigation of the accuracy of quotations in 150 articles printed in three biomedical journals. The authors' analysis of quotation errors "raises doubt in many cases that the original reference was read by the authors" (p. 1354).

In our research we found that rankings by citation counts are the most popular method for determining journal status in psychology. We located six studies in this area (Buss & McDermott, 1976; Garfield,

1975/1977; Haynes, 1983; Over, 1978; Rushton & Roediger, 1978; White & White, 1977).[4] However, each researcher employed a different method of selecting journals and/or means of assessing citation counts. Thus, the correlations between these studies are not impressively high. For example, the relationship between Buss and McDermott's ranking with that of White and White is .31 (Over, 1978). The relationship between White and White's list and that of Rushton and Roediger is .52 (Rushton & Roediger, 1978). Garfield's (1975) rankings correlate .77 with Buss and McDermott's list and .61 with White and White's ordering (Porter, 1978). Table 5 provides a list of the top 30 journals in studies where citation as the impact factor is used.

Also included in Table 5 is our combined ranking. This ranking was constructed by first making a list of all journals ranked in the six studies. Second, journals that were listed in at least three studies were included in the final combined ranking. Third, the average ranking for all eligible journals was calculated and a rank order of the top 30 journals was conducted. If authors are interested in having their work cited, being published in one of the journals ranked on the combined list in Table 5 enhances the odds of achieving that goal.

Impact of Subjective Prestige and Journal Rankings

Two studies have been conducted in which journals were rated on their subjective quality. Mace and Warner (1973) obtained ratings by department of psychology chairpersons on 64 journals. Koulack and Keselman (1975) had members of APA rate the top 100 journals in psychology. Again, the relationship between these two forms of journal rankings was low, $r = .36$ (Porter, 1978).

The rationale for the use of subjective rankings is that if significant professionals in the field are impressed with a journal's content, authors who publish in that journal will gain considerable prestige. The number of citations a journal engenders or other "objective" features on which a journal can be rated are less relevant than the actual judgments that influential professionals make regarding the quality of a given journal. In essence, the question becomes: Would authors prefer to be published in a journal judged to be of high quality by professionals although the article is unlikely to be cited, or have their article cited more often

---

[4]Matson et al.'s (1989) list of the top 57 journals, based on citation counts, is not included in this analysis due to questions raised by Howard et al. (1989) regarding how these rankings were derived.

Table 5
Top 30 Journals Rated by Citation Frequency[a]

Garfield's (1975) rankings

Psychological Review	Animal Behavior
Psychological Bulletin	Journal of Personality
Journal of Experimental Analysis of Behavior	Journal of Counseling Psychology
Journal of Experimental Psychology	Journal of Applied Psychology
Journal of Experimental & Social Psychology	Psychometrika
Journal of Personality & Social Psychology	Behaviour
Journal of Comparative & Physiological Psychology	British Journal of Psychology
Journal of Verbal Learning & Behavior	Psychonomic Science
Behaviour Research & Therapy	Psychophysiology
Canadian Journal of Psychology	Psychological Reports
Journal of Abnormal Psychology	Perceptual & Motor Skills
Journal of Consulting & Clinical Psychology	Journal of Psychology
Physiological Behavior	Child Development
Perception & Psychophysics	American Journal of Psychology
Journal of Educational Psychology	Journal of Social Psychology

---

Buss & McDermott's (1976) rankings

Journal of Experimental Psychology	Journal of Applied Psychology
Psychological Bulletin	Developmental Psychology
Journal of Abnormal Psychology	Journal of Personality
Psychological Review	Psychometrika
Journal of Comparative & Physiological Psychology	Perceptual & Motor Skills
American Psychologist	Journal of Experimental Child Psychology
Journal of Personality & Social Psychology	Psychophysiology
Science	British Journal of Psychology
Psychonomic Science	Psychological Monographs
Journal of Comparative & Clinical Psychology	Journal of Psychology

Table 5 (*continued*)

Journal of Verbal Learning & Behavior	American Journal of Psychiatry
Child Development	Journal of Educational Psychology
Journal of Experimental Analysis of Behavior	Journal of Social Psychology
Psychological Reports	Behaviour Research & Therapy
American Journal of Psychology	Journal of Experimental Social Psychology

White & White's (1977) rankings

Journal of Verbal Learning & Behavior	British Journal of Psychology
American Psychologist	Journal of Organizational Behavior & Human Performance
Journal of Applied Behavior Analysis	Monographs of the Society for Research in Child Development
Journal of Mathematical Psychology	Quarterly Journal of Experimental Psychology
Journal of Experimental Social Psychology	Journal of Abnormal Psychology
Psychological Bulletin	Personnel Psychology
Journal of Experimental Child Psychology	Behavior Research & Therapy
Child Development	Journal of Consulting & Clinical Psychology
Journal of Comparative & Physiological Psychology	American Journal of Psychology
Developmental Psychology	Journal of Counseling Psychology
Journal of Experimental Analysis of Behavior	Journal of Educational Measurement
Psychological Review	Journal of Experimental Psychology
	Journal of Personality & Social Psychology
	Canadian Journal of Psychology
	Journal of Applied Psychology
	Journal of Personality

Table 5 (*continued*)

Rushton & Roediger's (1978) rankings

Psychological Review
Cognitive Psychology
Psychological Bulletin
Journal of Verbal Learning & Behavior
Annual Review of Psychology
Vision Research
Psychophysiology
Journal of Experimental Analysis of
  Behavior
Journal of Experimental Child
  Psychology
Child Development
American Journal of Psychiatry

Journal of Comparative & Physiological
  Psychology
Developmental Psychology

Journal of the Acoustical Society of
  America
Learning & Motivation

Merrill-Palmer Quarterly
Perception & Psychophysics
Animal Behaviour
Memory & Cognition
Behaviour
American Psychologist
Journal of Experimental Psychology
Journal of Experimental Social
  Psychology
Behaviour Research & Therapy

Journal of Abnormal Psychology
Journal of Personality & Social
  Psychology
Quarterly Journal of Experimental
  Psychology
Journal of Child Psychology &
  Psychiatry and Allied Disciplines
Journal of Personality

Journal of Mathematical Psychology

Over's (1978) rankings

Psychological Review
Cognitive Psychology
Psychological Bulletin
Psychopharmacologia
Journal of Verbal Learning & Behavior
Annual Review of Psychology
Behavioral Biology
Physiology & Behavior
Psychophysiology
Journal of Experimental Analysis of
  Behavior
Journal of Experimental Child
  Psychology
Child Development
American Journal of Psychiatry

Psychosomatic Medicine
Learning & Motivation
Perception & Psychophysics
Animal Behavior
Memory & Cognition
Behaviour
Neuropsychologia
American Psychologist
Journal of Experimental Psychology
Journal of Experimental Social
  Psychology
Journal of Abnormal Psychology

Behaviour Research & Therapy
Journal of Personality & Social
  Psychology

Table 5 (*continued*)

Journal of Comparative Physiological Psychology	Quarterly Journal of Experimental Psychology
Developmental Psychology	Journal of Personality

Haynes' (1983) rankings

Progress in Behavior Modification	Journal of Experimental Social Psychology
Advanced Experimental Social Psychology	Psychophysiology
Annual Review of Psychology	Personnel Psychology
Advanced Clinical Child Psychology	Organizational Behavior & Human Performance
Psychology Review	Journal of Applied Psychology
Cognitive Psychology	Learning & Motivation
Journal of Verbal Learning & Behavior	Journal of Counseling Psychology
American Psychologist	International Journal of Clinical & Experimental Hypnosis
Journal of Personality & Social Psychology	Journal of Experimental Psychology: Human Learning & Memory
Memory & Cognition	Acta Psychologica
Journal of Abnormal Psychology	Journal of Comparative & Physiological Psychology
Journal of Experimental Psychology: General	Journal of Consulting & Clinical Psychology
Journal of Experimental Psychology: Human Perception & Performance	Journal of Personality
Psychological Bulletin	Journal of Abnormal Psychology
Journal of Experimental Psychology: Animal Behavior Processes	Journal of Educational Psychology

Combined rankings[b]

Psychological Review	Behaviour
Psychological Bulletin	Behaviour Research & Therapy
Journal of Verbal Learning & Behavior	British Journal of Psychology
Journal of Experimental Analysis of Behavior	Journal of Educational Psychology

Table 5 (*continued*)

Journal of Comparative & Physiological Psychology	Journal of Personality
Child Development	Canadian Journal of Psychology
American Psychologist	Journal of Applied Psychology
Psychophysiology	Psychometrika
Journal of Abnormal Psychology	American Journal of Psychiatry
Perception & Psychophysics	Quarterly Journal of Experimental Psychology
Journal of Personality & Social Psychology	American Journal of Psychology
Journal of Experimental Psychology	Journal of Counseling Psychology
Journal of Experimental Social Psychology	Psychological Reports
Animal Behavior	Perceptual & Motor Skills
Journal of Consulting & Clinical Psychology	Journal of Social Psychology

[a]Tied rankings among journals are not noted.
[b]Journal must be listed in three or more studies to be included.

although it is published in a journal considered by professionals to be of relatively low quality?

Several psychologists have taken issue with the subjective ratings of journal articles. Those advocating rankings based on citation obviously believe that this is a better method because an article that is cited, regardless of the journal that publishes it, receives a form of recognition. Second, journals listed high on citation rankings must have a high percentage of important articles. How else could these citation rates be explained?

Gynther (1973) argued that Mace and Warner's use of department chairpersons is a nonrepresentative sample. These individuals, he contended, tend to be experimentalists and their journal rankings reflect their bias. Boor (1973) added that ratings by department chairpersons (and presumably APA members) are more a product of journal familiarity than a valid measure of subjective judgment of quality. Adams and Peery (1980) presented the most embarrassing challenge to the use of subjective rankings. They noted that *Child Development Monographs* was ranked 19.5 in Mace and Warner's list of 64 journals and rated 37th on Koulack and Keselman's list of the top 100 journals. However, the last time that journal was published was in 1945!

The relationship between subjective journal rankings and that of journal rankings by citation ranges from .20 to .66. Mace and Warner's (1973) journal listings by department chairpersons correlated .66 with Buss and McDermott's (1976) and .56 with White and White's (1977) listings based on citation frequencies (Porter, 1978). Koulack and Keselman's (1975) subjective ratings by APA members correlated .38 with that of White and White's (1977) sample (Porter, 1978) and .20 with the citation listings of Rushton and Roediger (Rushton & Roediger, 1978). The degree of relationship between subjective measures of journal rankings with that of citation rankings is somewhat lower than the magnitude of the relationship between the various citation rankings with each other. The top 30 journals ranked by subjective preference are listed in Table 6.

Table 6 also includes a combined ranking, which was constructed by taking the average ranking for all APA journals common to both lists. For those journals included in only one list, a ranking of 101 was assigned as its second rank (Koulack and Keselman's list includes 100 journals) and its average was computed. For authors who hope to have their articles published in journals that psychologists believe are prestigious, a selection from the combined ratings of the top 30 journals listed in Table 6 is recommended.

Impact of Journal Circulation and Journal Rankings

In 1978 Ray Over suggested that subscription rates be considered an objective measure of a journal's importance. If large numbers of professionals purchase a journal, or receive a journal as part of their membership in an organization (e.g., the *American Psychologist*), it is likely that many articles in these journals will be read. If an author publishes in journals with relatively high circulation rates, name recognition will, presumably, follow. As of the preparation of this text no one to our knowledge has followed up on Over's idea, so we did. Utilizing the circulation figures published in *Journals in Psychology* (American Psychological Association, 1990), the top 30 journals were rank ordered by circulation rates as noted in Table 7.

When examining the listings in Table 7 it must be remembered these are circulation rates *reported* by the editors. There is no external verification. Also, inspection of these numbers indicates that the majority are estimates. It is obvious that journals do not have circulation rates in such nice round numbers.

Table 6
Top 30 Psychology Journals Ranked by Subjective Preference[a]

Mace & Warner's (1973) rankings

Journal of Comparative & Physiological Psychology	American Journal of Psychology
Journal of Personality & Social Psychology	British Journal of Psychology
Psychological Review	Journal of Organizational Behavior & Human Performance
Journal of Experimental Psychology	Science
Annual Review of Psychology	Child Development Monographs
Psychological Bulletin	Psychometrika
Developmental Psychology	Animal Behavior
Child Development	Journal of Experimental Social Psychology
Journal of Forensic Psychology	Journal of Experimental Research in Personality
Journal of Abnormal Psychology	Journal of Physiology
Scientific American	Psychological Monographs
American Psychologist	Journal of Mathematical Psychology
Biometrics	Human Factors
Journal of Verbal Learning & Behavior	Journal of Applied Psychology
Journal of Experimental Child Psychology	Journal of Experimental Analysis of Behavior

---

Koulack & Keselman's (1975) rankings

American Psychologist	Developmental Psychology
Psychological Bulletin	Journal of Experimental Psychology
Journal of Consulting & Clinical Psychology	Journal of Contemporary Psychology
Psychological Review	Journal of Educational Research
Journal of Abnormal Psychology	Journal of Humanistic Psychology
Psychology Today	Journal of Counseling Psychology
Science	Journal of Personality
Annual Review of Psychology	Psychotherapy: Theory, Research & Practice
Journal of Personality & Social Psychology	Journal of Comparative & Physiological Psychology
Journal of Educational Psychology	American Journal of Psychiatry

Table 6 (*continued*)

Mace & Warner's (1973) rankings

Journal of Clinical Psychology	Journal of Experimental Analysis of Behavior
Child Development	Professional Psychology
Journal of Applied Psychology	Journal of Educational Measurement
Scientific American	Behaviour Research & Therapy
Educational & Psychological Measurement	Journal of Experimental Social Psychology

Combined rankings

Psychological Review	Journal of Experimental Social Psychology
Psychological Bulletin	Journal of Experimental Child Psychology
Journal of Personality & Social Psychology	Child Development Monographs
Annual Review of Psychology	Journal of Experimental Analysis of Behavior
Journal of Abnormal Psychology	Psychology Monographs
American Psychologist	Journal of Verbal Learning & Behavior
Child Development	Journal of Organizational Behavior & Human Performance
Journal of Experimental Psychology	British Journal of Psychology
Developmental Psychology	Animal Behavior
Journal of Comparative & Physiological Psychology	Human Factors
Science	Journal of Experimental Research in Personality
Scientific American	Journal of Forensic Psychology
Journal of Applied Psychology	Biometrics
Psychometrika	Journal of Physiology
American Journal of Psychology	Journal of Mathematical Psychology

[a]Tied rankings not indicated.

Table 7
Top 30 Psychology Journals by Circulation

Journal	Circulation	Rank
American Psychologist	88,280	1
School Psychology Review	16,000	2
Journal of Mental Health Counseling	13,000	3
Family Process	12,000	4
American Journal on Mental Retardation	11,600	5
Journal of Consulting & Clinical Psychology	10,109	6
Child Development	8,500	7
Psychological Bulletin	7,590	8
Journal of Marriage & The Family	7,500	9
Clinical Psychology Review	6,500	11
International Journal of Group Psychotherapy	6,500	11
Psychotherapy	6,500	11
Australian Journal of Psychology	6,000	13.5
Psychological Perspectives	6,000	13.5
Psychological Review	5,963	15
Journal of Counseling Psychology	5,834	16
Australian Psychologist	5,800	17
Journal of Applied Psychology	5,653	18
Journal of Applied Behavior Analysis	5,613	19
Counseling Psychology	5,600	20.5
Monographs of the Society for Research in Child Development	5,600	20.5
Journal of Humanistic Psychology	5,593	22
Journal of Abnormal Psychology	5,450	23
Journal of Mental Imagery	5,321	24
Journal of Social Issues	5,224	25
Family Relations	5,200	26
Journal of Personality & Social Psychology	5,082	27
Counseling Education & Supervision	5,000	28.5
Transactional Analysis Journal	5,000	28.5
Canadian Psychologist	4,700	30

Some empirical support for the use of circulation rates as a viable measure of journal article status is provided by Haynes' (1983) research. Employing a technique used in physics, he endeavored to determine the most significant collection of journals in the field. To make this determination, termed a Discipline Impact Factor (DIF), the references cited in the core journals (rather than all journals in a field) are employed. Haynes considered the 16 APA journals as the core journals in psychology. From these 16 journals, references were made to 246 journals, of which the 31 highest cited journals were listed in his article. He also listed the citation frequency of these 31 journals using the traditional methods employed by Rushton and Roediger (1978) and White and White (1977).

Next, he computed seven predictor variables of both DIF and citation frequency listings. Two predictors were significant. The manuscript acceptance/rejection rate was negatively correlated for both listings, $-.38$ for the DIF method and $-.33$ for citation frequency. The second predictor variable to emerge was circulation rates, correlating .34 with DIF and .37 with citation frequency. When both predictors were combined, the two predictor variables correlated .52 with DIF and .50 with citation rankings.

A listing of a journal's circulation as an estimate of journal prestige seems comparable to an assessment of journal status based on citation rankings or subjective reputation. If authors desire to increase the probability that an article will be read, choosing to submit an article for publication in the top 30 journals listed in Table 7 is recommended.

The Combined Impact Factor and Journal Ratings

The three means of assessing journal prestige all have strengths and weaknesses. It is probably most desirable to generate a list of those journals that are rated high on all three impact factors. It is toward achieving this goal that Table 8 was constructed. Table 8 contains a list of all journals that are rated in the top 30 by citation, subjective judgment, and circulation impact. It also lists those journals that are rated in the top 30 on two of three impact factors.

If an article is published in a journal listed in Table 8 the author will be judged as being published in a high-quality journal, will have the article read by large numbers of psychologists, and will have it cited more often than most other papers.

Journal Ranking by Subfield

To increase the likelihood of being published in a better journal, it is advantageous to have information providing the maximum number of high-status journals that would be interested in an author's manu-

Table 8
Top Psychology Journals Ranked by Combined Ratings

Journals rated in top 30 in all three categories[a]	Journals rated in top 30 in two of three categories[a]
American Psychologist	American Journal of Psychology
Child Development	Animal Behavior
Developmental Psychology	British Journal of Psychology
Journal of Abnormal Psychology	Journal of Comparative & Physiological Psychology
Journal of Applied Psychology	Journal of Consulting & Clinical Psychology
Journal of Personality & Social Psychology	Journal of Counseling Psychology
Psychological Bulletin	Journal of Experimental Analysis of Behavior
Psychological Review	Journal of Experimental Psychology
	Journal of Experimental Social Psychology
	Journal of Verbal Learning & Behavior
	Psychometrika
	Psychophysiology

[a]Journals are listed in alphabetical order.

script. With this in mind, we prepared Table 9, which is a listing of the top journals in 10 subfields of psychology.

Feingold (1989) presented lists based on his preselection of 52 journals and a compilation of their citation frequencies for articles published in the 1985 and 1986 journal issues. Feingold's lists include the top five to nine journals in eight subdisciplines. Meltzer (1978) also used citation analysis based on eight articles' references in the 1970–1976 *Annual Review of Psychology* to determine the top 20 journals in personality psychology.

Table 9 includes the top 10 journals on Meltzer's list, as well as the top 10 listings for education journals based on Smart and Elton's (1981) study. These 10 journals are derived from citation analysis and account for 50% of all citations encountered in 148 journals of education. Peery and Adams' (1981) top 10 journals in child development are also listed in Table 9. These journals were selected by members of the Society for Research in Child Development (SRCD) ($N = 318$) as being the best in the field. Finally, Table 9 includes the top 10 journals rated as "most

Table 9
Top Journals in 10 Subfields of Psychology

Feingold's (1989) rankings

Applied psychology

Journal of Applied Psychology
Organizational Behavior & Human Decision Processes
Personnel Psychology
Journal of Vocational Behavior
Journal of Occupational Psychology
Human Relations
Journal of Occupational Behavior

Clinical/abnormal

Journal of Consulting & Clinical Psychology
Journal of Abnormal Psychology
Journal of Clinical Psychology
American Journal of Psychology
Psychotherapy

Feingold's (1989) rankings	*Peery & Adams' (1981) rankings*
Developmental	
Child Development	Child Development
Developmental Psychology	Developmental Psychology
Journal of Experimental Child Psychology	Journal of Experimental Child Psychology
Monographs of The Society for Research in Child Development	Merrill-Palmer Quarterly
Merrill-Palmer Quarterly	Human Development
Human Development	Monographs of The Society for Research in Child Development
Journal of Genetic Psychology	Journal of Genetic Psychology
International Journal of Behavioral Development	Psychological Bulletin
Child Study Journal	Psychological Review
	Cognitive Psychology

Table 9 (*continued*)

Smart & Elton's (1981) rankings

Educational

Child Development
Developmental Psychology
Journal of Educational Psychology
Journal of Applied Behavior Analysis
Journal of Counseling Psychology
American Journal of Mental Deficiency
Journal of Experimental Child Psychology
Journal of Genetic Psychology
Exceptional Children
Harvard Educational Review

Feingold's (1989) rankings

Experimental-learning & memory

Journal of Memory and Language
Journal of Experimental Psychology: Learning, Memory & Cognition
Journal of Experimental Psychology: General
Memory & Cognition
Quarterly Journal of Experimental Psychology
American Journal of Psychology
Bulletin of the Psychonomic Society
Psychological Research
Journal of General Psychology

Experimental-perception

Journal of Experimental Psychology: Human Perception & Performance
Journal of Experimental Psychology: General
Perception & Psychophysics
Perception
Bulletin of the Psychonomic Society
Psychological Research
Perceptual & Motor Skills

Table 9 (*continued*)

Feingold's (1989) rankings	Meltzer's (1978) rankings
Personality	
Journal of Personality & Social Psychology	Journal of Personality & Social Psychology
Journal of Personality	Journal of Consulting & Clinical Psychology
Personality & Social Psychology Bulletin	Psychological Reports
Personality & Individual Difference	Journal of Personality
Journal of Research in Personality	Psychological Bulletin
Journal of Personality Assessment	Journal of Abnormal Psychology
Social Behavior & Personality	Developmental Psychology
	Journal of Consulting Psychology
	Child Development
	Educational & Psychological Measurement

Feingold's (1989) rankings

Quantitative

Psychological Bulletin
Psychometrika
Multivariate Behavior Research
Educational & Psychological Measurement
Applied Psychological Measurement

McKee's (1988) rankings

School

School Psychology Review
Journal of School Psychology
Psychology in the Schools
Journal of Psychoeducational Assessment
Professional School Psychology
Journal of Learning Disabilities
Exceptional Children
Education & Treatment of Children

Table 9 *(continued)*

Journal of Special Education
Child Development

Feingold's (1989) rankings

Social

Journal of Personality & Social Psychology
Journal of Experimental Social Psychology
Personality & Social Psychology Bulletin
Social Psychology Quarterly
European Journal of Social Psychology
Journal of Applied Social Psychology
Journal of Social Psychology
Basic & Applied Social Psychology
Social Behavior & Personality

useful" by members of the National Association of School Psychologists (McKee, 1988).

A perusal of the journals listed in Table 9 indicates that most overlap considerably with the journals listed in our composites presented in Tables 5, 6, 7, and 8. If authors want to publish articles in journals that appeal directly to researchers in a given specialty of psychology, submission to one of the journals listed in Table 9 should be considered.

Using Author's Guides

At this point authors should have some idea regarding which of several high impact journals may be receptive to their manuscript. However, there remains the question of which specific journals would be interested in the topic and whether the manuscript conforms to those journals' specifications (i.e., page limitations, writing style, APA, Chicago Manual of Style). Likewise, there are the very basic questions of to whom one should submit the manuscript, the editor's address, and how many copies to forward. Other vital information includes the time it will take for the manuscript to be reviewed, any cost associated with being published in the journal, etc. Because recognition of one's publication is considered essential (at least to readers who agree with our position), it is important to know which abstracts (*Psychological Ab-*

stracts, ERIC, Medical Index) summarize articles published in the respective journals. And it is, of course, important to have data available on a journal's circulation rate.

Fortunately, all of this information and more is available in the author's guides to journals in the behavioral sciences. Three author's guides are available: *Author's Guide to Journals in Psychology, Psychiatry and Social Work* (JPPSW) (Markle & Rinn, 1977), *Author's Guide to Journals in the Behavioral Sciences* (AGJBS) (Wang, 1989), and *Journals in Psychology* (JP) (American Psychological Association, 1990). Each guide is evaluated below against 12 areas of information we deem helpful in assisting authors in their selection of journals for manuscript submission.

1. *Types of manuscripts accepted*: A description is provided on preferable content areas, including describing desired subjects (child development, application of learning theories, etc.) and what method of presentation is appropriate (i.e., experimental versus qualitative discussion). JPPSW does best in this area, with 97% of its listings having information in this category. JP also does well, with 92% of its listings providing this information. However, only 68% of the journals listed in AGJBS provide this information.

2. *High-status journals listed*: The types of manuscript accepted by each journal listed in Table 8 are presented. JPPSW describes the type of manuscripts accepted by all 20 of these journals; for JP this figure is 90%, and for AGJBS the type of manuscript accepted by 70% of these journals is listed.

3. *Percentage of manuscripts accepted*: This percentage provides authors with an estimate of the chances of their submission being accepted for publication. Ninety-two percent of the journals listed in AGJBS provide this information, 80% of the journals listed in JPPSW have these data, whereas only 3% of the journals presented in JP contain information in this category.

4. *Circulation rate*: An editor's reported circulation frequency, per each issue of the journal, is presented. JPPSW provides this information on 89% of the journals listed, for AGJBS 78% of the journals provide circulation rates, and for JP 76% of the journals provide this information.

5. *Manuscript style*: A statement is made regarding what written format is acceptable (e.g., APA, Chicago). Some journals allow more than one format. For those publications listed, 88% of JPPSW entries

contain information in this category, 81% of AGJBS listings have this information, and for JP 79% of the journals provide these data.

6. *Page limitations*: Information regarding the maximum number of typed pages allowed is presented. AGJBS provides such data on 93% of its journal listings. In JP, only 2% of the journals include this information, and for JPPSW none of this information is available.

7. *Peer review journals*: A statement is made that informs whether or not each listed journal utilizes peer review. Again, almost none of the listings in JPPSW and only 1% of listings in JP provide this information, whereas 96% of the journals in AGJBS provide it.

8. *Lag time from submission to notification*: The time it takes from submission until the time it takes to notify an author of acceptance/ rejection is recorded. For AGJBS, 92% of the journals include these data; for JPPSW 88% have this information, but only 2% of the journals listed in JP report such data.

9. *Lag time from acceptance to publication*: Once a paper is accepted for publication (usually after several revisions) there is a time span before the article reaches print. This information is provided for 97% of the journals in AGJBS and 90% of the journals in JPPSW. Only 1% of the journals in JP give this estimate.

10. *Cost of publishing and/or purchasing reprints*: If there is a charge to authors for the cost of publication or agreement to purchase reprints of the published article, this information needs to be known prior to submission. Ninety-six percent of the journals listed in JPPSW provide this information, 69% of AGJBS listings do likewise, whereas only 5% of JP entries have these data.

11. *Abstracts listed*: A list is presented for each journal regarding what abstract service provides summaries for articles published. Usually, the more abstracts that summarize a journal's articles, the more likely an article will be noticed by researchers who review the literature. Ninety-two percent of JPPSW's listings contain this information, 46% of AGJBS listings do also, but none of the journals listed in JP attend to this category at all.

12. *Name of journal editor and address of where to submit the manuscript*: This is extremely critical information and 100% of all journals listed in the three author's guides have this information. However, the date of publication for the author's guide becomes important in providing current names of journal editors and their address. For example, JPPSW is a 1977 publication and cannot be expected to have up-to-date

Table 10
Percent of Author's Guides Listings for 12 Categories of Information

Categories	Author's guides		
	JPPSW[a]	AGJBS[b]	JP[c]
Types of manuscripts accepted	97[d]	68	92
High-status journals	100	70	90
Percent of manuscripts accepted	80	92	03
Circulation rate	89	78	76
Manuscript style	88	81	79
Page limitations	00	93	02
Peer review	00	96	01
Lag time: Submission-notification	88	92	02
Lag time: Acceptance-notification	90	97	01
Cost to publish	96	69	05
Abstracts listed	92	46	00
Name of editor/address	100	100	100

[a]*Author's Guide to Journals in Psychology, Psychiatry, and Social Work* (Markle & Rinn, 1977).
[b]*Author's Guide to Journals in the Behavioral Sciences* (Wang, 1989).
[c]*Journals in Psychology* (American Psychological Association, 1990).
[d]All numbers expressed as percents.

information. To be on the safe side, it is strongly suggested that once a set of journals has been selected for potential manuscript submission, the researcher go directly to the journal page where instructions to prospective authors are given and follow the guidelines. A summary of the 12 categories and the percentage of journal listings that provide information in each category is presented in Table 10.

The preferred sequence for determining which of the better journals may be receptive to a manuscript is the following:

1. Before preparing a manuscript, author's guides should be consulted. A list of all journals that publish articles utilizing the format in which the manuscript is prepared (experimental study, professional issues discussion, etc.) and focussing on the topic researched should be prepared.

2. References appearing in the manuscript and the citations used by those articles referenced should be examined. By consulting author's guides, a determination can be made re-

garding which journals can be added to the list of potential journals for submission.

3. From the tentative list of journals generated from following steps #1 and #2 above, refer to Table 8. Those journals that are named in Table 8 and appear on the tentative list should be the journals selected for submission.

4. If there is no overlap between the tentative list of journals and those contained in Table 8, one should explore overlap of the list generated with those journals included in Tables 5, 6, 7, and 9. Select for submission among those journals that are included in the Tables and on the tentative list.

5. Once the selection has been narrowed to a few journals, it is important to obtain a copy of each journal's instructions to authors. The final list of journals should then be rank ordered. Based on the journal selected, the manuscript should be written in accordance with that journal's specifications and submitted for publication.

6 RECOMMENDATIONS FOR SYSTEMIC CHANGE

The plethora of irrelevant studies in the journal publication process can best be viewed as evidence of a systemic problem. The judgments and behaviors of three interconnected groups have produced and maintained this situation. These three groups are university personnel, journal editors and reviewers, and scientist/authors. Changes in policies are recommended for each group. These suggested alterations are considered realistic and do not require great effort or considerable commitment of funds. If implemented, they could lead to substantial improvement in the quality of published scientific data.

Recommended Changes for University Personnel

As discussed in Chapter One, there is strong reason to believe that a considerable proportion of poor quality research is directly attributable to the publish or perish policy of many universities and/or academic departments. Quantity of publications appears to serve several evaluative functions, including the determination of who is hired and promoted and who obtains tenure. Thousands of teachers and researchers may be forced to publish something—anything—to survive professionally. There is no evidence that the publish or perish policy has contributed to momentous discoveries nor has it resulted in the accumulation of valuable knowledge in the behavioral sciences. As Boice and Jones (1984) reported, 10% of scientists account for 50% of the published literature. Many of the remaining 50% only publish enough to fulfill university/department publication criteria.

The use of publication counts to evaluate universities, departments, or individuals in terms of status, prestige, and promotion is actually an abdication of judgment. If the criterion for institutional status and/or promotion of an individual is simply the number of publications, obviously little or no evaluation of quality is being made. Publication counts are objective and reliable in the sense that administrators can add and, thus, can determine the number of journal publications that staff members have to their credit. (It is, of course, recognized that different formulas exist for determining publication credit on the basis of type of publication—journal article, book, etc.—and on the number of authors involved.)

Given the number of journals publishing articles in the behavioral sciences, coupled with data indicating that about 75% of manuscripts are ultimately accepted for publication, the measurement of the numbers of papers in print is best viewed as an estimate of a researcher's motivation. Professors who do not meet the publish or perish guideline cannot be accused of failing to contribute to science because most articles make little or no contribution in any event. An argument can be made that these professionals are indirectly facilitating science by not clogging the publication system with frivolous studies.

It appears that for some university departments, the use of publication counts as an unbiased measure of faculty competence reduces stress for those responsible for making evaluations. Deans, department chairpersons, and tenure-granting committees can avoid blame (or legal action) by relinquishing their duty to make judgments of a colleague's abilities by making decisions based on publication production. Often difficult and/or unpopular decisions have to be made regarding a professional's skills. Efforts should be directed to the development of instruments that assess article quality, teaching excellence, community involvement, and contribution to department/university functioning (Boyer, 1990). It is granted that agreement among evaluators will not be high; however, neither is agreement among peer reviewers. If those responsible for evaluating others worry about the accusation of bias, it may be possible to establish a reciprocal relationship with other universities for the purpose of evaluating personnel in areas of hiring, firing, promotion, and tenure.

If publish or perish practices disappear, there is no reason to believe the behavioral sciences will suffer. There is no doubt that fewer papers will be submitted and a noticeable percentage of journals will probably be terminated. But this should not necessarily be interpreted as a negative outcome. Broad and Wade (1982b) affirmed our contention that "what is needed is greater competition brought about by a sharp reduction in the number of journals" (p. 222). The majority of universities currently in existence performed scientific research and educated students satisfactorily long before the popularity of the publish or perish policy. A return to the evaluation of faculty performance in the "good old days" is by no means necessarily regressive.

A second area in which university policies can play a direct role is in the reduction of the potential for fraudulent behavior. In order to prevent fraud and possible embarrassment to the university and to scientific endeavor in general, it is important for research institutions to prepare and distribute written documents governing ethical scientific conduct. More significantly, universities should develop and enact specific practices that prevent or detect fraud. Although no one wishes to put obstacles in the way of doing research—there are enough already—it is imperative that methods of experimentation and data collection be as free of bias as possible. Parapsychologists have become accustomed to constant scientific questioning of their procedures and data-gathering techniques and are very aware of the need to police their publications. Scientists in other fields are enjoined to be as vigilant.

In order to reduce the incidence of bias and fraudulent behavior, it is suggested that universities consider forming groups of research scientists, one of whose functions would be to audit the experiments of others. These audits could be random and involve members of departments where overlap in expertise exists. For example, a committee of psychologists, biologists, and sociologists could be charged with the responsibility of auditing studies conducted by the department of psychology. For a chemistry department, such a committee might be composed of members of the department of chemistry, physics, and biology.

Another possibility would be to form a working relationship between several universities located in a convenient geographical area. A committee of psychologists from one university could be responsible for auditing research conducted in another university's psychology department and vice versa. Some professors may complain about their academic freedom being threatened. However, the purpose of auditing committees would not be to judge the appropriateness of a study, but to assess whether procedures, data collection, and data analysis had been undertaken in a manner consistent with recognized scientific standards.

Recommended Changes for Editors/Reviewers

In order to reduce dramatically the number of inconsequential studies published, journal editors and peer reviewers must take steps to eliminate the biases that plague research efforts (i.e., the almost exclusive demand for statistical significance testing, the persistent refusal to publish replication studies and negative findings, as well as confirmatory bias). Following are some of the ways in which editors may reduce the impact of these biases.

Editors and peer reviewers should insist that authors analyze their data with more meaningful statistics than significance tests. Meehl (1986) complained that "it is scandalous that editors still accept manuscripts in which authors present tables of significance tests without giving measures of overlap [or other useful information]" (p. 334). In this text we have advocated the use of confidence intervals, measures of accounted-for variance, and ES. However, we are in agreement with Carver's (1978) conclusion that "the use of statistical tests of significance is not likely to decline until one or more journal editors speak against statistical significance testing" (p. 397). We are at a loss as to why editors cannot relinquish this type of useless—even possibly deceptive—method of data analysis. We are tempted to believe that they may be convinced that they are providing what their reading audience expects.

On the other hand, as previously noted, editors have been very generous in their publication of articles criticizing the use of statistical significance testing. Editors, however, in spite of the fact that they are uniquely positioned to do so, do not seem willing to take that ostensibly drastic step. The use of such methods cannot be supported through logical argument, empirical demonstration, or practicality of outcome. Our only hope is that a group of editors of prestigious journals will *simultaneously* change their policy toward such tests, and adopt more meaningful statistics.

The only prospect for overcoming the bias against publishing replications is to have some mechanism by which performing and publishing replication studies are built into the journal publication system. It is proposed that editors of high-status journals take the lead in providing a specified percentage of their journal space for replication research. Cummings and Frost (1985) suggested that 10% of journal space be devoted to replication studies. Bornstein (1991b) suggested that APA allow 2% of its journal articles to be replication studies in the form of two- to three-page brief reports. This would result in approximately 100 published replications per year. Lamal (1991) even proposed that an entire journal in the social sciences be directed to replication research.

Regardless of whether an entire journal or a proportion of pages within a journal is allocated to replications, the credibility and reader interest in such experiments would be enhanced if high-status authors were invited to undertake such studies. For example, reading about B. F. Skinner's replication of Festinger's cognitive dissonance experiment should generate considerable interest.

Another possibility would be to bring together authors who have studied the same area but have produced conflicting data. These authors, in conjunction with a well-respected moderator, could be invited to cooperate on some mutually agreed upon experiments that replicate each other's work. The prototype of this method was employed when Locke arbitrated a series of four experiments developed by Lathan and Erez and published the results in the *Journal of Applied Psychology Monographs*. These studies were initiated because Lathan and Erez were both studying goal setting but were reporting highly discrepant findings. When the three scientists analyzed their results, they discovered that the inconsistencies in experimental outcome were a direct result of procedural differences in the methodology (Frost & Stablein, 1992). Their paper won an award for the best article in the Organizational Behavior Division of the Academy of Management.

Examination of data related to bias against publishing studies reporting negative outcomes and that of confirmatory bias points to one specific problem—reviewers often judge the quality of an entire study on the basis of the research findings. We pointed out that when reviewers are not privy to the results, manuscripts are often rated as comparable in quality to those where reviewers have access to the findings and where the outcome is statistically significant and/or confirms the reviewer's theoretical position. The best demonstration of this dynamic was Mahoney's (1977) data in which referees who had the experimental findings available and where the results were in concert with their theoretical preferences gave these manuscripts a mean rating of 4.3 for the paper's scientific contribution. Reviewers not having access to the results assigned a mean rating of 4.5 to the same manuscripts. For referees assessing the scientific contribution of the same manuscripts in which the results disconfirmed their theoretical bias, the mean rating declined to 2.4. The experimental outcome affected reviewers' ratings of the Methods section and, of course, the final recommendation to accept or reject for publication. Our recommendation, therefore, is to have reviewers judge an article's quality without the Results and Discussion sections being provided.

It is proposed that experimental and quasi-experimental manuscripts be written in the same form as currently outlined in the APA *Publication Manual* (third edition, 1983) with the expectation that the Results and Discussion sections are not submitted. Once the manuscript is accepted for publication, then the Results and Discussion sections are forwarded to the editor. Instead of submitting the results, it is suggested that authors submit a Results section that outlines what statistical procedures will be employed to analyze each hypothesis. The argument being made is that if a study has focused on a relevant topic, and if the experimenter has provided a sound rationale, used satisfactory sample selection with methodological and procedural vigor, and proposed appropriate statistical analysis, then the results of the study are apt to be informative regardless of outcome. It is also suggested that anonymous review continue as is. (Kupfersmid, 1988, p. 640)

This recommendation has been made by a variety of researchers in the behavioral sciences for over 20 years (Lane & Dunlap, 1978; Mahoney, 1977; Sterling & Jang, 1988; Walster & Cleary, 1970). Kupfersmid (1988) listed 10 advantages of this procedure over that of the current system.

1. The number of pages of a manuscript needing to be reviewed would be reduced because the Results and Discussion sections would be unavailable. This would also lessen the lag time between manuscript submission and author notification.

2. The time it takes an author to write a manuscript would be reduced because data analysis would not have to be performed and the Results and Discussion sections would not have to be submitted.

3. Authors would receive feedback regarding their manuscript's publication acceptance/rejection before data analysis. Thus, the temptation to perform an almost infinite

number of statistical analyses in search of a few statistically significant *p* values would be diminished.

4. Editors and reviewers could concentrate their efforts on the relevancy of the topic, sample selection, and appropriateness of the experimental design. Thus, research quality should improve.

5. Because editors and reviewers would not know the experimental outcome, the "file drawer/Type I error" problem would be reduced.

6. Not knowing the research outcome would encourage editors' and reviewers' receptivity to more meaningful statistical analysis, such as confidence intervals, coefficients of determination, and ES scores.

7. There should be less pressure on researchers to distort data to reach acceptable *p* values because the submission would not be judged on this dimension.

8. Perhaps replication studies would be more acceptable to editors and reviewers because statistical significance testing would no longer be involved.

9. With the elimination of the Discussion section, there might be less reason for authors to engage in long discourses about the importance of their study to all areas of psychology.

10. Because judgment of the manuscript would not be influenced by the experimental results, there may be greater agreement among reviewers regarding the quality of submissions.

These suggestions, of course, have their critics. Clarke (1990) claimed that statistical significance testing is the only objective aspect of a research study and if it were eliminated only subjective characteristics of a manuscript would be left to be assessed. He concluded that this would result in lowered interrater agreement on the quality of a manuscript. Whether lower interrater agreement would occur is testable. Furthermore, statistical significance is, itself, a subjective phenomenon. The alpha level is determined by the experimenter and, even if set by tradition at .05, would still not qualify as objective.

Subjective aspects of a research study include what to study, how to design the study, what subjects should be included, how many subjects are to be measured, what statistics to use, etc. If Clarke can tolerate all other facets of research being subjective, why is there something sacrosanct about a significance test? If he concedes that setting an alpha level is subjective, but believes that the success or failure to reach this level is objective, there is partial agreement. There is an objective factor in determining whether a significance level is achieved, but what is more critical is how (subjectively) meaningful this bit of data is.

Clarke, citing Chow (1988), contended that the use of statistics that measure effect size is appropriate for descriptive research but that tests of statistical significance are appropriate for experiments that attempt to corroborate explanatory theories. Problems with Chow's position were delineated in Chapter Two.

Clarke also contended that if the Results section were not submitted, authors would be less likely to engage in more meaningful data analysis because such effort would have no effect on the decision of an editor to publish a study. He seems to have missed the point. Editors tend to accept for publication studies that employ statistical significance testing and, almost exclusively, those that report statistically significant outcomes. As a consequence, researchers almost always submit manuscripts that conform to this editorial procedure and place in the "file drawer" studies where the outcomes are not statistically significant. This practice results in a ubiquitous Type I error contamination in psychology's data banks and greatly restricts data analysis to only one form—statistical significance testing.

Perhaps Meehl said it best: "The almost universal reliance on merely refuting the null hypothesis as the standard method for corroborating substantive theories in the soft areas is a terrible mistake, is basically unsound, poor scientific strategy, and one of the worst things that ever happened in the history of psychology" (Meehl, 1978, p. 817).

Ozorak (1990) expressed concern that if the Results section were not submitted, researchers would not be held accountable for an interpretation of the data. We believe all scientists hold investigators responsible for providing reasonable interpretations of their experimental findings. The format proposed does not alter this responsibility. However, the proposal does change the *time* at which an experimenter is responsible for data interpretation. The current system evaluates the researcher's interpretation *prior to* publication acceptance or rejection. Our recommendation places this responsibility on a researcher *after* (conditional) publication acceptance.

Another concern is that researchers would perform the data analysis regardless of whether a Results and Discussion section was part of the submission process, thus time would not be saved. It is believed that even if these two sections were omitted, the length of manuscripts submitted for publication would not be reduced (Clarke, 1990). We agree that the majority of researchers would analyze their data even if the peer review process did not initially require submission of the Results and Discussion sections. But, not having to *write* these two sections prior to acceptance of a manuscript would save time on the part of both the author and the peer reviewer(s).

We fail to understand how the elimination of the writing or reading of two sections of a study would be just as time consuming as if these two sections were included. Additionally, how a manuscript without the submission of a Results and Discussion section could be equal in length to manuscripts that include these two sections escapes us. We are not suggesting that editors alter their standards regarding the upper limit on the number of total pages (which includes the Results and Discussion section in the final draft) allowable for review. They could simply limit the number of pages allowable for a first submission of a manuscript in which the Results and Discussion sections were not included.

Three further concerns are grouped together because our reply, it is hoped, will simultaneously mitigate these anxieties. First, there is some fear that peer reviewers may be reluctant to judge manuscripts without the inclusion of the Results section (Crandall, 1990); second, editors may not be clear on what they are reviewing in the absence of these two sections; and third, writing style would suffer because students are taught to write about an experiment keeping the Results section in mind (Clarke, 1990).

It is normal to feel some trepidation with the introduction of a new method into an established system. Some of this anxiety may be alleviated by recognizing that the proposal is *not new* to science in general, or psychology in particular. It is only new to the evaluation of journal articles. A doctoral candidate's dissertation is primarily evaluated by assessing the study's rationale, sampling method, and experimental procedure. Doctoral candidates are not supposed to be evaluated on the basis of whether their results are statistically significant. If an entire discipline (as well as all of science) is willing to confer its highest degree without depending on an experimental outcome, surely these same professionals are capable of making judgments about the quality of other studies without knowledge of the results.

Millions of dollars in grant funds are awarded every year to scientific disciplines. Committees of experts from each field, specialty, and sub-specialty within a field evaluate many proposals. Yet, very few protest that this money is being spent on financing studies *prior* to knowledge of the outcome. Although it seems ridiculous to make such a statement (because if the outcome were known there would be no need for the study), the point is that scientists routinely make decisions on the value of a study without knowledge of results. Furthermore, how would a lack of knowledge of an experimental outcome change the style of a research report in a negative direction? Clarke seems to be confused as to who is privy to the results and who is not. The author has access to his or her own findings, the editor/reviewer does not. How then would style be compromised?

Lastly, Ozorak (1990) argued that not submitting the Results and Discussion sections ignores the pressure to publish that young scholars face. She noted that academicians must conform to the standards editors and peer reviewers set in order to get published. Ozorak seems to misunderstand who the audience for this proposal is. The purpose of this recommendation is to convince *editors* to alter their behavior.

Clarke (1990) stated that if the Results and Discussion sections were not submitted, it would be very difficult to include multiple experiments in one manuscript. We agree, and suggest that submission of multiple experiments does require a Results section. We believe, however, that the benefits of adopting our recommendation for the majority of studies outweigh its liabilities, but this can only be judged after data are collected and evaluated. Fiske and Fogg's (1990) research on the lack of agreement when analyzing the free response comments of peer reviewers indicated that the absence of the Results and Discussion pieces would not increase the degree of agreement. They reported that the most common criticisms of a manuscript are in the categories that address the interpretation of the data and the conclusions made after data analysis.

There is, in point of fact, a possible weakness in our proposal that has gone unnoticed by the critics. This criticism is that the global rating of agreement between reviewers for acceptance or rejection of a manuscript usually results in interrater correlations in the .30s range (see Table 2), whereas ratings of agreement between referees on the importance of the topic and quality of the experimental design range in the .20s (see Table 3). Thus, in the absence of the Results section there may be reason to assume that agreement between peer reviewers will decline.

Whether reviewer reliability increases, decreases, or remains unchanged as a function of implementing our proposal is, of course, open to empirical investigation. We believe that a large part of the unaccounted-for variance in interrater agreement is directly attributable to the effect that experimental findings have on influencing a reviewer's judgment in many areas of rating manuscript quality. This position is also open to experimental inquiry.

As editor of the *Journal of Social Behavior and Personality*, Crandall has been actively studying the journal publication process. He (1990) and Clarke (1990) agreed that our recommendation is sufficiently worthwhile to implement for the purpose of evaluation. Two editors have initiated the process. The *International Journal of Forecasting* presents authors with the option of submitting a manuscript without inclusion of the Results section. *Advanced Psychological Measurement* extends to authors the choice of utilizing their Advanced Review Option (Weiss, 1989) which closely resembles the structure of our proposal.

A concern that some may have with our position is that the biomedical field does make progress and is rife with discovery, despite the fact that its journals exhibit the same type of negative features as do journals in the behavioral sciences. Biomedical journals often show the same reliance on the use of statistical significance testing and publish few replication studies and little negative outcome research. Similarly, the interrater reliability among reviewers of biomedical journals is comparable to that in psychology journals.

We believe that the same journal publication practices that are detrimental for psychology are also harmful for the biomedical field. However, biomedicine has been able to overcome these barriers because of one critical factor—it is easier to detect important discoveries in biomedicine than in the behavioral sciences. It is relatively uncomplicated to determine if a particular organism is responsible for a disease; it is usually simple to measure the degree to which a treatment prolongs life; and the extent of improvement a medication has over a placebo is often quite straightforward. When something is discovered in most areas of medicine that has potential benefit, the signal is loud and is clearly heard over the noise. In psychology it is much more difficult to differentiate between the wheat and the chaff.

There are several characteristics of biomedical research that increase the likelihood that an important discovery will stand out among trivial findings.

1. In biomedical studies, the measurements of dependent variables are often clearly valid indices. If a treatment (independent variable) has an effect on reducing cancer cell formation and/or increasing length of survival (dependent variables), nobody questions the importance of these dependent variables and/or whether cancer cell formation or life expectancy is a valid measure. However, in psychology, a treatment that has a positive effect on increasing intelligence, reading comprehension, and/or emotional well-being suffers from potential criticism directed at both the measurement of the independent and dependent variable(s). The construct validity of variables is a constant concern. In biomedicine, the relationship of a dependent variable to reality is almost never an issue.

2. In biomedical areas, a relevant finding can be detected even when a difference between a control group and a treatment group is quite small. As previously noted, Rosenthal (1990) demonstrated how an r = .034 can be shown to indicate that ingestion of aspirin has an important role to play in the prevention of heart attacks. To the best of our knowledge, nowhere in the history of psychology or education has a correlation of .034 been reported where the researcher smiled with delight over such a "consequential" finding. In the biomedical field a small positive effect on a salient dependent variable can have far-reaching implications. Members of the psychological profession have difficulty agreeing on the implications when large effects (i.e., correlations in the .5 and over range) are found, with small effects essentially being ignored.

3. The methods of measurement in biomedicine are often far superior to those in psychology. Although no measurement is free from error, biomedical instrumentation is often much less subject to human error and bias than that in psychology. Subjective factors of the examiner and the participant often greatly limit the conclusions and generalizations that can be made in a psychological investigation. This is less of a factor in biomedical research. Biomedical instrumentation allows for greater precision of measurement. The degree of precision and depth of measurement that can be gleaned from the electron microscope's peek into the workings of a neuron or that of the non-obtrusive glimpse magnetic resonance imaging produces is impressive. There is no device in psychology that approaches the sophistication of

these instruments. Psychologists are still trying to invent their first microscope.

Recommended Changes for Authors

Strategies that an author can take to publish quality papers have been the major focus of this book. The contents of Chapter Four spelled out specific ways in which behavioral scientists can enhance researching and writing manuscripts that address topics of importance. The guidelines presented in Chapter Four are summarized below:

1. Concentrate effort on the important topics in a field. Ask the fundamental questions and concentrate on experimental designs that can potentially contribute to an answer.

2. Design studies such that either a positive or negative outcome will have meaningful implications.

3. Use accepted experimental procedures. If you depart from this guideline, be prepared to provide a lengthy logical argument and empirical support for this deviation. Be sure that measures for independent and dependent variable(s) have demonstrated reliability and validity.

4. A *representative*, not an *available*, sample should be employed. Subjects should be comparable to the population to which the researcher desires to generalize. Research on treatment techniques usually requires clinical samples. College students are a poor substitute. Research on child development should employ children in a range of abilities and social classes, rather than university-based elementary and high school students. If college students or university school children are employed as subjects, researchers should *convincingly* justify the sample selection to the journal readership.

5. It is unfortunately essential to analyze data via statistical significance testing because editors/reviewers are not yet ready to dispense with this procedure. However, data should also be analyzed through the use of confidence intervals, coefficients of determination, and/or ES. Engaging in the above practices should not negatively affect editors' or reviewers' evaluations.

6. It cannot be stressed enough that persistence gets results, whether this refers to sticking to investigating an important area and/or having a paper on a significant topic published.

If research efforts are concentrated on generating large numbers of publications, that goal will probably be achieved. However, it is very unlikely that such a focus will result in significant discoveries. The best way to discover something important is to go looking for it. The second best way is through serendipity (i.e., accidental discovery). Even these findings, though, are most apt to occur when a researcher has been open to investigating an unexpected phenomenon because its relevance to fundamental questions is appreciated.

If our recommendations are followed, publication practices in the 21st century will be quite different from those that currently exist. Yet, earth-shattering changes are not required in journal operations, or at the university and/or departmental level. Furthermore, author behavior toward conducting research and writing manuscripts will remain essentially intact.

A Fantasy

It is our dream that in the 21st century the policy of publish or perish will be nonexistent at most universities. Those who enjoy performing research will have the opportunity to do so as part of their job. Because most scientists presumably enjoy research (or they would have probably chosen some other profession), experimental studies will continue to flourish, but there will be a noticeable reduction in the number of manuscripts submitted for publication.

This reduction will be a direct result of two factors. One is that researchers will spend more time establishing experimental designs and collecting representative samples. This will mean more time and energy will be devoted to the conducting of each individual experiment. Greater pains will be taken to focus on critical concerns and to generate readily interpretable data. This will reduce the number of studies a researcher can perform over a given time period. Second, many professors who do not enjoy research will not be doing it for the purpose of job advancement and/or promotion. These individuals may have a greater teaching load and perform more service to the community, their students, and to the functioning of their academic department.

Universities will have written policies regarding ethical aspects of the research process. There will be inter- and intradepartmental research auditing committees. Some of these committees will be composed of professionals employed at the same university. Others will involve faculty of different universities, while still a third group will be composed of a mixture of individuals from both within and outside a given institution. Members of these committees will inspect experiments that are in process or have been completed.

Rather than seeing this as an intrusion on academic freedom, researchers will view audits as a method of assuring the academic community—as well as the public at large—that their laboratory conducts research that is creditable and analyzes data impartially. Professors will feel proud when an audit concludes that their laboratory is functioning in accordance with recognized scientific principles. University deans, department heads, and other administrators will take pride in the manner in which science is conducted under their leadership.

This redistribution of individuals' publications will result in many faculty being able to spend more time preparing for their classes, whereas others will spend a greater amount of time preplanning research projects. It is anticipated that both knowledge gained by students and information gained from research will be enhanced. With this change in priorities, many universities will want to maintain a balance between those primarily engaged in research and those whose principal function is teaching.

A university that employs an overabundance of researchers may get the reputation of being an institution that does not care about its students, or the educational process in general. If this occurs, undergraduate enrollment may drop. A university that has a reputation for good teaching but which is not at the forefront of discovery may have a hard time drawing graduate students. *However, a university that has acquired name recognition for both quality teaching and research will have little trouble attracting students or faculty.* It may be expected that a good teaching reputation will attract good teachers and encourage ordinary teachers to improve. Similarly, good researchers may inspire more quality studies.

With the decline in the amount of research being done, there will be a reduction in the number of papers submitted for publication. With the increased length of time needed to perform a study, each researcher will produce fewer studies per year. Also, there will be no need to divide an investigation into the least publishable unit. The drop in the number of submissions will probably result in many journals ceasing to exist. Of the 300 journals currently publishing articles in the behavioral sciences, a third to one half may not operate in the 21st century. However, the remaining 150 journals will be sufficient to accommodate all of the meaningful research in the field.

Manuscripts submitted to publishers will be shorter. The Results and Discussion sections will not be included as part of the original submission. Thus, the time it takes for an author to write a manuscript and an editor/reviewer to read it and make a decision will be appreciably reduced. Once a paper is accepted for publication the Results and Discussion sections will be submitted. The length of these two sections will be shorter than those written in the 20th century. There will be little temptation to perform a near infinite number of statistical analyses in search of a statistically significant p value in the Results section. The Discussion section will also contain fewer pages because the need to relate a study to all areas of human functioning will be lessened.

Confidence intervals, measures of accounted-for variance, and ES will dominate the types of statistical analyses performed on variables. By the accumulation of studies, a better estimate of a variable's range of values, magnitude of effect, and degree of covariance will be possible, allowing scientists to predict more accurately human and animal functioning.

In the 21st century most journals will devote a percentage of pages to publishing replication studies. Often, an editor will ask a distinguished scientist to perform the replication. Such a request from an editor will be a form of recognition of one's status in the field. Lesser-known experimentalists will perform replication research and submit their findings. If such replications are published, lesser-known scientists will be enhancing their reputations.

Because the research outcome does not affect a manuscript's probability of being published and because replications will be commonplace, it will take considerably less time and fewer studies will be necessary to accumulate support or nonsupport for theories of psychological functioning. In the 20th century it is routine to read a review of literature that involves a summary of hundreds of investigations. No longer will it be necessary for so many investigations to be conducted in a given area—for so many repetitions of essentially the same study—for such a profusion of questionably valid material.

Scientists will be more satisfied with the progress in their field and more confident in the correctness of their findings. This increase of confidence in the research literature will result in greater implementation of diagnostic and treatment strategies based on experimental findings. Such enactment of improved techniques by practitioners will create a feedback loop to experimentalists regarding what findings are clinically worthwhile and which require modification. This informal system of collaboration will generate an appreciable improvement in the validity and comprehensiveness of theories and techniques in the behavioral sciences. More accurate theories, coupled with more effective diagnostic and treatment techniques, will result in more effective programs for the prevention and treatment of physical and psychological problems.

As noted in Chapter One, the goal of this text is to improve the way in which scientific studies are conducted and reported. As can be seen from our view of the future, we have not placed conservative restrictions on our vision. Most recommendations, however, emphasize changes in thinking, rather than doing (though much remains to be done). Attitudes regarding the publish or perish policy for universities and biases regarding statistical significance testing and the publication of negative results and replication studies in the peer review system are some of the most formidable obstacles to improving the quality of scientific reporting.

We are aware of the fact that current publication practices have been sustained because, like popular paradigms in science, there have been no convincing systems to supplant them. Therein lies both our optimism and our pessimism. It is hoped that the contents of this text will encourage at least a few university research committees and editors of professional journals to evaluate their position on the issues addressed and that they will seriously consider the proposals that have been made.

REFERENCES

Adair, R. (1982). A physics editor comments on Peters and Ceci's peer-review study. *Behavioral and Brain Sciences, 5*, 196.

Adams, G., & Peery, J. (1980). If you can name it, I can rank it. *American Psychologist, 35*, 109–110.

Adler, T. (1989, June). Scientific fraud: How to handle it? *APA Monitor*, p. 5.

Adler, T. (1991, December). Outright fraud rare, but not poor science. *APA Monitor*, p. 11.

American Psychological Association. (1983). *Publication manual of the American Psychological Association*. Washington, DC: Author.

American Psychological Association. (1988). *Journals in psychology*. Washington, DC: Author.

American Psychological Association. (1990). *Journals in psychology* (3rd ed., rev.) Washington, DC: Author.

American Psychological Association Committee on Women in Psychology. (1980). A survey of the selection of reviewers of manuscripts for psychology journals. *American Psychologist, 35*, 1106–1110.

Amir, Y., & Sharon, I. (1991). Replication research: A "must" for the scientific advancement of psychology. In J. Neuliep (Ed.), *Replication research in the social sciences* (pp. 51–69). Newbury Park, CA: Sage.

Angell, M. (1989). Negative studies. *The New England Journal of Medicine, 321*, 464–466.

Armstrong, J. (1982). Research on scientific journals. Implications for editors and authors. *Journal of Forecasting, 1*, 83–104.

Atkinson, D., Furlong, M., & Wampold, B. (1982). Statistical significance, reviewer evaluations, and the scientific process: Is there a (statistically) significant relationship? *Journal of Counseling Psychology, 29*, 189–194.

Bakan, D. (1966). The test of significance in psychological research. *Psychological Bulletin, 66*, 423–437.

Barlow, D. (1981). On the relation of clinical research to clinical practice: Current issues, new directions. *Journal of Consulting and Clinical Psychology, 49*, 147–155.

Barlow, D., Hays, S., & Nelson, R. (1984). *The scientist practitioner: Research and accountability in clinical and educational settings.* New York: Pergamon Press.

Berardo, F. (1980). Publish or perish: Some guidelines for the novice. *The Southern Sociologist, 11*, 3–7.

Bernard, H. (1982). Computer-assisted referee selection as a means of reducing potential editorial bias. *Behavioral and Brain Sciences, 5*, 202.

Boice, R., & Jones, F. (1984). Why academicians don't write. *Journal of Higher Education, 55*, 567–582.

Boor, M. (1973). Unfamiliarity breeds disdain: Comment on department chairmen's ratings of psychological journals. *American Psychologist, 28*, 1012–1013.

Bornstein, R. (1991a). The predictive validity of peer review: A neglected issue. *Behavioral and Brain Sciences, 14*, 138–139.

Bornstein, R. (1991b). Publication politics, experimenter bias and the replication process in social science research. In J. Neuliep (Ed.), *Replication research in the social sciences* (pp. 71–81). Newbury Park, CA: Sage.

Boyer, E. (1990). *Scholarship reconsidered: Priorities of the professoriate.* Princeton, NJ: The Carnegie Foundation for the Advancement of Teaching.

Bozarth, H., & Roberts, R. (1972). Signifying significant significance. *American Psychologist, 27*, 774–775.

Bracey, G. (1987, March 25). The time has come to abolish research journals: Too many are writing too much about too little. *The Chronicle of Higher Education*, p. 44.

Bradley, J. (1981). Pernicious publication practices. *Bulletin of the Psychonomic Society, 18*, 31–34.

Bradley, J. (1982). Editorial overkill. *Bulletin of the Psychonomic Society, 19*, 271–274.

Broad, W. (1981). The publishing game: Getting more for less. *Science, 211*, 1137–1139.

Broad, W., & Wade, N. (1982a, December). Betrayers of the truth. *The Ambassador*, pp. 39–46, 48, 50.

Broad, W., & Wade, N. (1982b). *Betrayers of the truth.* New York: Simon & Schuster.

Buss, A., & McDermott, J. (1976). Ratings of psychology journals compared to objective measures of journal impact. *American Psychologist, 31*, 675–678.

Cameron, L. (Speaker). (1990). *How to publish your manuscripts* (Tape #90–246). Washington, DC: American Psychological Association.

Campbell, J. (1985). Editorial: Some remarks from the outgoing editor. In L. Cummings & P. Frost (Eds.), *Publishing in the organizational sciences* (pp. 321–333). Homewood, IL: Richard D. Irwin. (Original work published 1982)

Carver, R. (1978). The case against statistical significance testing. *Harvard Educational Review, 48*, 378–399.

Ceci, S., & Peters, D. (1984). How blind is blind review? *American Psychologist, 39*, 1491–1494.

Chalmers, I., Adams, M., Dickersin, K., Hetherington, J., Tarnow-Mordi, W., Meinert, C., Tonascia, S., & Chalmers, T. (1990). A cohort study of summary reports of controlled trials. *Journal of the American Medical Association, 263*, 1401–1405.

Chow, S. (1988). Significance test or effect size? *Psychological Bulletin, 103*, 105–110.

Cicchetti, D. (1980). Reliability of reviews for the *American Psychologist*: A biostatistical assessment of the data. *American Psychologist, 35*, 300–303.

Cicchetti, D. (1991). The reliability of peer review for manuscript and grant submissions: A cross-disciplinary investigation. *Behavioral and Brain Sciences, 14*, 119–135.

Clarke, J. (1990). Comments on Kupfersmid. *American Psychologist, 45*, 666–667.

Cohen, J. (1988). *Statistical power analysis for the behavioral sciences*. Hillsdale, NJ: Lawrence Erlbaum.

Cohen J. (1990). Things I have learned (so far). *American Psychologist, 45*, 1304–1312.

Cohen L. (1979). The research readership and information source reliance of clinical psychologists. *Professional Psychology, 10*, 780–785.

Cohen, L., Sargent, M., & Sechrest, L. (1986). Use of psychotherapy research by professional psychologist. *American Psychologist, 41*, 198–206.

Cole, S. (1991). Consensus and the reliability of peer-review evaluations. *Behavioral and Brain Sciences, 14*, 140–141.

Cole, S., Cole, J., & Simon, G. (1981). Chance and consensus in peer review. *Science, 214*, 881–886.

Coursol, A., & Wagner, E. (1986). Effect of positive findings on submission and acceptance rates: A note on meta-analysis bias. *Professional Psychology: Research and Practice, 17*, 136–137.

Cowen, E., Spinell, A., Hightower, A., & Lotyczewski, B. (1987). Author reactions to the manuscript revision process. *American Psychologist, 42*, 403–405.

Cowles, M., & Davis, C. (1982). On the origins of the .05 level of statistical significance. *American Psychologist, 37*, 553–558.

Cox, W., & Catt, V. (1977). Productivity ratings of graduate programs in psychology based on publications in the journals of the American Psychological Association. *American Psychologist, 32*, 793–813.

Craig, J., & Reese, S. (1973). Retention of raw data: A problem revisited. *American Psychologist, 28*, 723.

Crandall, R. (1978). Interrater agreement of manuscripts is not so bad! *American Psychologist, 33*, 623–624.

Crandall, R. (1987). We need research on what constitutes good journal papers—and good editing—not guesswork on how to improve manuscripts! *American Psychologist, 42*, 407–408.

Crandall, R. (1990). Improving editorial procedures. *American Psychologist, 45*, 665–666.

Crane, D. (1967). The gatekeepers of science: Some factors affecting the selection of articles for scientific journals. *American Sociologist, 2*, 195–201.

Creswell, J. (1985). *Faculty research performance: Lessons from the sciences and social sciences* (ASHE-ERIC Higher Education Report No. 4). The George Washington University, One Dupont Circle, Suite 630, Washington, DC.

Cummings, L., & Frost, P. (1985). Conceptual perspective. In L. Cummings & P. Frost (Eds.), *Publishing in the organizational sciences* (pp. 3–13). Homewood, IL: Richard D. Irwin.

Cummings, L., Frost, P., & Vakil, T. (1985). The manuscript review process: A view from the inside on coaches, critics, and special cases. In L. Cummings & P. Frost (Eds.), *Publishing in the organizational sciences* (pp. 469–508). Homewood, IL: Richard D. Irwin.

Dooling, D., & Danks, J. (1975). Going beyond tests of significance: Is psychology ready? *Bulletin of the Psychonomic Society, 5*, 15–17.

Eaton, W. (1984). On obtaining unpublished data for research integrations. *American Psychologist, 39*, 1325–1326.

Editors. (1992, January 3). Information for contributors. *Science*, pp. 36–38.

Eichorn, D., & VandenBos, G. (1985). Dissemination of scientific and professional knowledge: Journal publication within the APA. *American Psychologist, 40*, 1309–1316.

Endler, N., Rushton, J., & Roediger, H. (1978). Productivity and scholarly impact (citations) of British, Canadian, and U.S. departments of psychology (1975). *American Psychologist, 33*, 1064–1082.

Engler, R., Covell, J., Friedman, P., Kitcher, P., & Peters, R. (1987). Misrepresentation and responsibility in medical research. *The New England Journal of Medicine, 317*, 1383–1389.

Evans, J., Nadjari, H., & Burchell, S. (1990). Quotational and reference accuracy in surgical journals. *Journal of the American Medical Association, 263*, 1353–1354.

Eysenck, H. (1980). Editorial. *Personality and Individual Differences, 1*, 1–2.

Feingold, A. (1989). Assessment of journals in social science psychology. *American Psychologist, 44*, 961–964.

Finke, R. (1990). Recommendations for contemporary editorial practices. *American Psychologist, 45*, 669–670.

Fisher, K. (1982, November). The spreading stain of fraud. *APA Monitor*, pp. 1, 7–8.

Fiske, D., & Fogg, L. (1990). But the reviewers are making different criticisms of my paper! *American Psychologist, 45*, 591–598.

Fletcher, J. (1991). Journal availability and the quality of published research. *Behavioral and Brain Sciences, 14*, 146–147.

Freund, J. (1960). *Modern elementary statistics.* Englewood Cliffs, NJ: Prentice Hall.

Friedman, P. (1990). Correcting the literature following fraudulent publication. *Journal of the American Medical Association, 263*, 1416–1419.

Frost, P., & Stablein, R. (1992). *Doing exemplary research.* Newbury Park, CA: Sage.

Garfield, E. (1972). Citation analysis as a tool in journal evaluation. *Science, 178*, 471–479.

Garfield, E. (1977). Journal citation studies. 19. Psychology and behavior journals. In E. Garfield (Ed.), *Essays of an information scientist* (pp. 231–235). Philadelphia, PA: iSi Press. (Original work published 1975)

Garfield, E., & Welljams-Dorof, A. (1990). The impact of fraudulent research on the scientific literature. *Journal of the American Medical Association, 263*, 1424–1426.

Garvey, W., & Griffith, B. (1971). Scientific communication: Its role in the conduct of research and creation of knowledge. *American Psychologist, 26*, 349–362.

Garvey, W., & Griffith, B. (1979). Communication and information processing within scientific disciplines: Empirical findings for psychology. In W. Garvey (Ed.), *Communication: The essence of science* (pp. 127–147). Oxford, England: Pergamon Press.

Garvey, W., Lin, N., & Tomita, K. (1979). Research studies in patterns of scientific communications: III, Information-exchange processes associated with the production of journal articles. In W. Garvey (Ed.), *Communication: The essence of science* (pp. 202–224). Oxford, England: Pergamon Press.

Ghiselin, M. (1989). *Intellectual compromise: The bottom line.* New York: Paragon House.

Goodstein, L., & Brazis, K. (1970). Credibility of psychologists: An empirical study. *Psychological Reports, 27*, 835–838.

Gordon, L. (1991, March). More teaching, less research in Stanford president's plan. *Akron Beacon Journal*, p. 4A.

Gottfredson, S. (1978). Evaluating psychological research reports: Dimensions, reliability, and correlates of quality judgements. *American Psychologist, 33*, 920–933.

Greenwald, A. (1975). Consequences of prejudice against the null hypothesis. *Psychological Bulletin, 82*, 1–20.

Greenwald, A. (1976). An editorial. *Journal of Personality and Social Psychology, 33*, 1–7.

Greenwald, A. (1987). Comments on "The publication game." *Journal of Social Behavior and Personality, 2*, 13–22.

Gynther, M. (1973). On Mace and Warner's journal ratings. *American Psychologist, 28*, 1013.

Harlow, H. (1962). Fundamental principles for preparing psychology journal articles. *Journal of Comparative and Physiological Psychology, 55*, 893–896.

Haynes, J. (1983). An empirical method for determining core psychology journals. *American Psychologist, 38*, 959–961.

Hedges, L. (1987). How hard is hard science, how soft is soft science? *American Psychologist, 42*, 443–455.

Hedrick, T., Boruch, R., & Ross, J. (1978). On ensuring the availability of evaluative data for secondary analysis. *Policy Sciences, 9*, 259–280.

Henkel, R. (1976). *Tests of significance*. Newbury Park, CA: Sage.

Hoaglin, D., & Andrews, D. (1975). The reporting of computation-based results in statistics. *American Statistician, 29*, 122–126.

Hostetler, A. (1987a, November). The case of science ethics v. libel. *APA Monitor*, pp. 16–17.

Hostetler, A. (1987b, May). Investigation: Fraud inquiry revives doubt: Can science police itself? *APA Monitor*, pp. 1–2.

Hostetler, A. (1987c, November). Many researchers see, speak no evil. *APA Monitor*, p. 16.

Hostetler, A. (1987d, July). NIMH sends fraud case to justice. *APA Monitor*, p. 18.

Howard, G., Cole, D., & Maxwell, S. (1989). On productive and unproductive: Comments about productivity. *American Psychologist, 44*, 739–741.

Humphreys, L. (1980). The statistics of failure to replicate: A comment on Buriel's (1978) conclusions. *Journal of Educational Psychology, 72*, 71–75.

Hunt, K. (1975). Do we really need more replications? *Psychological Reports, 36*, 587–593.

Jensen, A. (1992). Scientific fraud or false accusations? The case of Cyril Burt. In D. Miller & M. Hersen (Eds.), *Research fraud in the behavioral and biomedical sciences* (pp. 97–123). New York: John Wiley.

Kamin, L. (1974). *The science and politics of I.Q.* New York: John Wiley.

Kendall, P., & Ford, J. (1979). Reasons for clinical research: Characteristics of contributors and their contributions to the *Journal of Consulting and Clinical Psychology*. *Journal of Consulting and Clinical Psychology, 47*, 99–105.

Kerr, S., Tolliver, J., & Petree, D. (1977). Manuscript characteristics which influence acceptance for management and social science journals. *Academy of Management Journal, 20*, 132–141.

Knoll, E. (1990). The communities of scientists and journal peer review. *Journal of the American Medical Association, 263*, 1330–1332.

Korn, J., & Bram, D. (1988). What is missing in the method section of APA journal articles? *American Psychologist, 43*, 1091–1092.

Koulack, D., & Keselman, H. (1975). Ratings of psychology journals by members of the American Psychological Association. *American Psychologist, 30*, 1049–1053.

Kupfersmid, J. (1988). Improving what is published: A model in search of an editor. *American Psychologist, 43*, 635–642.

Kupfersmid, J., & Fiala, M. (1990). *A survey of attitudes and behaviors of authors who publish in psychology and educational journals.* Unpublished manuscript.

Kupfersmid, J., & Fiala, M. (1991). A survey of attitudes and behaviors of authors who publish in psychology and education journals. *American Psychologist, 46*, 249–250.

Lamal, P. (1991). On the importance of replication. In J. Neuliep (Ed.), *Replication research in the social sciences* (pp. 31–35). Newbury Park, CA: Sage.

Lane, D., & Dunlap, W. (1978). Estimating effect size: Bias resulting from the significance criterion in editorial decisions. *British Journal of Mathematical Statistics in Psychology, 31*, 107–112.

Lewicki, P. (1982). Social psychology as viewed by its practitioners: Survey of SESP members' opinions. *Personality and Social Psychology Bulletin, 8*, 409–416.

Lindsey, D. (1977). Participation and influence in publication review proceedings: A reply. *American Psychologist, 32*, 579–586.

Lindsey, D. (1978). *The scientific publication system in social science.* San Francisco: Jossey-Bass.

Lipsey, M. (1974). Research and relevance: A survey of graduate students and faculty in psychology. *American Psychologist, 29*, 541–553.

Lock, S., & Smith, J. (1990). What do peer reviewers do? *Journal of the American Medical Association, 263*, 1341–1343.

Lykken, D. (1970). Statistical significance in psychological research. In D. Morrison & R. Henkel (Eds.), *The significance test controversy* (pp. 267–279). Chicago: Aldine. (Original work published 1968)

Mace, K., & Warner, H. (1973). Ratings of psychology journals. *American Psychologist, 28*, 184–187.

Maher, B. (1978). A reader's, writer's, and reviewer's guide to assessing research reports in clinical psychology. *Journal of Consulting and Clinical Psychology, 46,* 835–838.

Mahoney, M. (1976). *Scientists as subject: The psychological imperative.* Goleta, CA.: Health Science Systems, P.O. Box 2485.

Mahoney, M. (1977). Publication prejudices: An experimental study of confirmatory bias in the peer review system. *Cognitive Therapy and Research, 1,* 161–175.

Mahoney, M. (1979). Psychology of the scientist: An evaluative review. *Social Studies of Science, 9,* 349–375.

Mahoney, M. (1985). Open exchange and epistemic progress. *American Psychologist, 40,* 29–39.

Mahoney, M. (1987). Scientific publication and knowledge politics. *Journal of Social Behavior and Personality, 2,* 165–176.

Mahoney, M., Kazdin, A., & Kenigsberg, M. (1978). Getting published. *Cognitive Therapy and Research, 2,* 69–70.

Markle, A., & Rinn, R. (1977). *Author's guide to journals in psychology, psychiatry & social work.* New York: Haworth Press.

Marsh, H., & Ball, S. (1981). Interjudgmental reliability of reviews for the *Journal of Educational Psychology. Journal of Educational Psychology, 73,* 877–880.

Matson, J., Gouvier, W., & Manikam, R. (1989). Publication counts and scholastic productivity: Comment on Howard, Cole, and Maxwell. *American Psychologist, 44,* 737–739.

McCartney, J. (1976). Confronting the journal publication crisis: A proposal for a council of social science journal editors. *American Sociologist, 11,* 144–152.

McGraw, K., & Wong, S. (1992). A common language effect size statistic. *Psychological Bulletin, 111,* 361–365.

McKee, W. (1988). The book tells more than its cover: A reply to Bracken. *School Psychology Review,* 17, 366–369.

McNutt, R., Evans, A., Fletcher, R., & Fletcher, S. (1990). The effects of blinding on the quality of peer review. *Journal of the American Medical Association, 263,* 1371–1376.

Meehl, P. (1978). Theoretical risks and tabular asterisks: Sir Karl, Sir Ronald, and the slow progress of soft psychology. *Journal of Consulting and Clinical Psychology, 46,* 806–834.

Meehl, P. (1986). What social scientists don't understand. In D. Fiske & R. Shweder (Eds.), *Metatheory in the social sciences: Pluralism and subjectivity* (pp. 315–338). Chicago: University of Chicago Press.

Meltzer, H. (1978). Ratings of journals by and for personality psychologists. *American Psychologist, 33,* 776–777.

Merton, R. (1973). The Matthew effect in science. In N. Storer (Ed.), *The sociology of science: Theoretical and empirical investigations* (pp. 439–459). Chicago: University of Chicago Press. (Original work published 1963)

Mitchell, T., Beach, L., & Smith, K. (1985). Some data on publishing from authors' and reviewers' perspectives. In L. Cummings & P. Frost (Eds.), *Publishing in the organizational sciences* (pp. 248–264). Homewood, IL: Richard D. Irwin.

Mohr, L. (1990). *Understanding significance testing.* Newbury Park, CA: Sage.

Morrison, D., & Henkel, R. (1969). Significance tests reconsidered. *American Sociologist, 4,* 131–140.

Morrison, D., & Henkel, R. (1970). Significance tests in behavioral research: Skeptical conclusions and beyond. In D. Morrison & R. Henkel (Eds.). *The significance test controversy* (pp. 305–311). Chicago: Aldine. (Original work published 1969)

Morrow-Bradley, C., & Elliot, R. (1986). Utilization of psychotherapy research by practicing psychotherapists. *American Psychologist, 41,* 188–197.

Myers, C. (1970). Journal citations and scientific eminence in contemporary psychology. *American Psychologist, 25,* 1041–1048.

Neher, A. (1967). Probability pyramiding, research error and the need for independent replication. *The Psychological Record, 17,* 257–262.

Nelson, K. (1982). Reliability, bias or quality: What is the issue? *Behavioral and Brain Sciences, 5,* 229.

Nisbett, R. (1978). A guide for reviewers: Editorial hardball in the '70's. *American Psychologist, 33,* 519–520.

Nobel, J. (1990). Comparison of research quality guidelines in academic and nonacademic environments. *Journal of the American Medical Association, 263,* 1435–1437.

Over, R. (1978). Journal rankings by citation analysis: Some inconsistencies. *American Psychologist, 33,* 778–780.

Ozorak, E. (1990). Response to "Improving what is published": A model in search of writers. *American Psychologist, 45,* 667.

Peery, J., & Adams, G. (1981). Qualitative ratings of human development journals. *Human Development, 24,* 312–319.

Perlman, D. (1982). Reviewer "bias": Do Peters and Ceci protest too much? *Behavioral and Brain Sciences, 5,* 231–232.

Peters, D., & Ceci, S. (1982). Peer-review practices of psychological journals: The fate of published articles, submitted again. *Behavioral and Brain Sciences, 5,* 187–195.

Pfeifer, M., & Snodgrass, G. (1990). The continued use of retracted, invalid scientific literature. *Journal of the American Medical Association, 263,* 1420–1423.

Porter, A. (1978). A comparison of the various ratings of psychology journals. *American Psychologist, 33,* 295–299.

Rennie, D. (1986). Guarding the guardians: A conference on editorial peer review. *Journal of the American Medical Association, 256*, 2391–2392.

Rennie, D. (1990). Editorial peer review in biomedical publication. *Journal of the American Medical Association, 263*, 1317.

Richmond, S. (1964). *Statistical analysis.* New York: The Ronald Press.

Riordan, C., & Marlin, N. (1987). Some good news about some bad practices. *American Psychologist, 42*, 104–106.

Rodman, H. (1970). Notes to an incoming journal editor. *American Psychologist, 25*, 269–273.

Roediger III, H. (1987). The role of journal editors in the scientific process. In D. Jackson & J. Rushton (Eds.), *Scientific excellence: Origins and assessment* (pp. 222–252). Beverly Hills, CA: Sage Foundation.

Rosenthal, R. (1978). How often are our numbers wrong? *American Psychologist, 33*, 1005–1008.

Rosenthal, R. (1979). The "file drawer problem" and tolerance for null results. *Psychological Bulletin, 86*, 638–641.

Rosenthal, R. (1990). How are we doing in soft psychology? *American Psychologist, 45*, 775–777.

Rosenthal, R. (1991a). *Meta-analytic procedures for social research.* Newbury Park, CA: Sage.

Rosenthal, R. (1991b). Replication in behavioral research. In J. Neuliep (Ed.), *Replication research in the social sciences* (pp. 1–30). Newbury Park, CA: Sage.

Rosenthal, R. (1991c). Some indices of the reliability of peer review. *Behavioral and Brain Sciences, 14*, 160–161.

Rosenthal, R., & Rubin, D. (1979). A note on percent of variance explained as a measure of the importance of effects. *Journal of Applied Social Psychology, 9*, 395–396.

Rosenthal, R., & Rubin, D. (1982). A simple, general purpose display of magnitude of experimental effect. *Journal of Educational Psychology, 74*, 166–169.

Rowney, J., & Zenisek, T. (1980). Manuscript characteristics influencing reviewers' decisions. *Canadian Psychology, 21*, 17–21.

Rozeboom, W. (1960). The fallacy of the null-hypothesis significance test. *Psychological Bulletin, 57*, 416–428.

Rushton, J., & Roediger III, H. (1978). An evaluation of 80 psychology journals based on the *Science Citation Index. American Psychologist, 33*, 520–523.

Salsburg, D. (1985). The religion of statistics as practiced in medical journals. *The American Statistician, 39*, 220–223.

Samelson, F. (1980). J. B. Watson's Little Albert, Cyril Burt's twins, and the need for a critical science. *American Psychologist, 35*, 619–625.

Schaeffer, D. (1970). Do APA journals play professional favorites? *American Psychologist, 25*, 362–365.

Sechrest, L. (1987). Approaches to ensuring quality of data and performance: Lessons for science? In D. Jackson & J. Rushton (Eds.), *Scientific excellence: Origins and assessment* (pp. 253–283). Beverly Hills, CA: Sage Foundation.

Sedlmeier, P., & Gigerenzer, G. (1989). Do studies of statistical power have an effect on the power of studies? *Psychological Bulletin, 105*, 309–316.

Shadish, W. (1989a). The perception and evaluation of quality in science. In B. Gholson, W. Shadish, R. Neimeyer, & A. Houts (Eds.), *Psychology of science: Contributions to metascience* (pp. 383–426). Cambridge: Cambridge University Press.

Shadish, W. (1989b). Science evaluation: A glossary of possible contents. *Social Epistemology, 3*, 189–204.

Simes, R. (1987). Confronting publication bias: A cohort design for meta-analysis. *Statistics in Medicine, 6*, 11–29.

Smart, R. (1964). The importance of negative results in psychological research. *Canadian Psychologist, 5*, 225–232.

Smart, J., & Elton, C. (1981). Structural characteristics and citation rates of education journals. *American Educational Research Journal, 18*, 399–413.

Smith, M. (1980). Publication bias and meta-analysis. *Evaluation in Education, 4*, 22–24.

Smith, M., Glass, G., & Miller, T. (1980). *The benefits of psychotherapy*. Baltimore: The Johns Hopkins University Press.

Smith, N., Jr. (1970). Replication studies: A neglected aspect of psychological research. *American Psychologist, 25*, 970–975.

Sommer, B. (1987). The file drawer effect and publication rates in menstrual cycle research. *Psychology of Women Quarterly, 11*, 233–242.

Spencer, N., Hartnett, J., & Mahoney, J. (1986). Problems with reviewers in the standard editorial practice. *Journal of Social Behavior and Personality, 1*, 21–36.

Sterling, T. (1970). Publication decisions and their possible effects on inferences drawn from tests of significance or vice versa. In D. Morrison & R. Henkel (Eds.), *The significance test controversy* (pp. 295–300). Chicago: Aldine. (Original work published 1959)

Sterling, T., & Jang, K. (1988). *The effect of the outcome of statistical tests on the decision to publish*. Unpublished manuscript, School of Computing Science, Faculty of Applied Sciences, Simon Fraser University, Burnaby, B. C., Canada V5A 1S6.

Thelen, M., & Rodriquez, M. (1987). Attitudes of academic and applied clinical psychologists towards training issues 1969–1984. *American Psychologist, 42*, 412–415.

Thompson, B. (1988). A note about significance testing. *Measurement and Evaluation in Counseling Development, 20*, 146–148.

Thorne, F. (1977). The citation index: Another case of spurious validity. *Journal of Clinical Psychology, 33*, 1157–1161.

Tighe, T. (1979). A new publication policy. *American Psychologist, 34*, 720–722.

Tversky, A., & Kahneman, P. (1971). Belief in the law of small numbers. *Psychological Bulletin, 76*, 105–110.

Tyrer, P. (1991). Chairman's action: The importance of executive decisions in peer review. *Behavioral and Brain Sciences, 14*, 164–165.

Walster, G., & Cleary, T. (1970). A proposal for a new editorial policy in the social sciences. *The American Statistician, 24*, 16–19.

Wang, A. (1989). *Author's guide to journals in the behavioral sciences.* Hillsdale, NJ: Lawrence Erlbaum.

Ward, A., Hall, B., & Schramm, C. (1975). Evaluation of published educational research: A national survey. *American Educational Research Journal, 12*, 109–128.

Watson, J., & Rayner, R. (1920). Conditional emotional reactions. *Journal of Experimental Psychology, 3*, 1–14.

Weiss, C., & Bucuvalas, M. (1980). *Social science research and decision-making.* New York: Columbia University Press.

Weiss, D. (1989). An experiment in publication: Advanced publication review. *Applied Psychological Measurement, 13*, 1–7.

Weller, A. (1990). Editorial peer review in US medical journals. *Journal of the American Medical Association, 263*, 1344–1347.

White, M., & White, K. (1977). Citation analysis of psychology journals. *American Psychologist, 32*, 301–305.

Whitehurst, G. (1984). Interrater agreement for journal manuscript reviews. *American Psychologist, 39*, 22–28.

Wolf, F. (1986). *Meta-analysis.* Newbury Park, CA: Sage.

Wolff, W. (1973). A study of criteria for journal manuscripts. *American Psychologist, 28*, 257–261.

Wolins, L. (1962). Responsibility for raw data. *American Psychologist, 17*, 657–658.

Wonderly, D. (1991). *Motivation, behavior, and emotional health: An everyman's interpretation.* New York: University Press of America.

Wong, P. (1981). Implicit editorial policies and the integrity of psychology as an empirical science. *American Psychologist, 36*, 690–691.

Wyer, R., Greenwald, A., Bernard, H., Crandall, R., & Anon. (1987). Comments on "The publication game." *Journal of Social Behavior and Personality, 2*, 13–22.

Yankauer, A. (1990). Who are the peer reviewers and how much do they review? *Journal of the American Medical Association, 263*, 1338–1340.

Zuckerman, H., & Merton, R. (1971). Patterns of evaluation in science: Institutionalisation, structure and functions of the referee system. *Minerva, 9*, 66–100.

INDEX